Reminiscences and Recipes of Early Big Thicket Boarding Houses

BOARDIN' · IN · THE THICKET

Wanda A. Landrey

Foreword by Francis Edward Abernethy

University of North Texas Press

Printed in the United States of America

First Edition, 1990

Requests for permission to reproduce material from this work should be sent to the University of North Texas Press, P.O. Box 13856, Denton, Texas 76203-3856

Library of Congress Cataloging-in-Publication Data

Boardin' in the Thicket: reminiscences and recipes of early Big Thicket boarding houses / Wanda A. Landrey
     p.   cm.
Includes bibliographical references.
ISBN 0-929398-07-6
1. Hotels, taverns, etc.—Texas—Big Thicket—History.
2. Cookery, American—Texas style.   3. Big Thicket (Tex.)—Social life and customs.   I. Title.
TX909.L36   1990
647.94764'1403—dc20   89-24868
                                                              CIP

Cover Design by Richard M. Kohen, Shadow Canyon Graphics
Interior Design and Typography by Shadow Canyon Graphics,
  Evergreen, Colorado

TABLE OF CONTENTS

Foreword xi
Acknowledgements xv
Preface xvii

Kountze: The Commercial Hotel 1
  Recipes 6
    Chicken Pot Pie 6
    Sweet Potato Casserole 7
    Jam Cake, Filling, Icing 8
    Egg Custard Pie 9
    Red-Eye Gravy 10
    Beef Tea 11

Sour Lake: The Springs Hotel Resort 13
  Recipes 21
    Pan-Fried Venison 22
    Dried Venison 22
    Venison Roast 23
    Venison Chili 23
    Squirrel Stew 24
    Squirrel and Dumplings 25
    Roast Duck, Squirrel, or Goose 26
    Bear Meat 27

Silsbee: The Badders Hotel/The City Hotel 29
  Recipes 40
    Mrs. Badders Steamed Fruitcake 40
    Ginger Cookies 42
    Mrs. Nixson's Chili Beans 43
    Yeast Rolls 44
    French-Fried Onions 45
    Butter Cake 45

Southeast Texas: The Harvey Houses 47
  Recipes 52
    A Zesty Appetizer 53
    Tomato-Cheese Salad 53
    Clam Chowder 54
    Creamed Stuffed Eggs 55
    White Sauce 55
    Cheese Biscuits 55
    Corned Beef Hash 56
    Corned Beef Hash and Eggs 57
    Cheese Soufflé 57
    Beef Rissoles with Mashed Potatoes 58
    Mashed Potatoes 58
    Brown Gravy 59
    Mayonnaise 60
    Pecan Torte, Filling, Icing 61

Bessmay: The Bessmay Hotel 63
  Recipes 68
    Stew 68
    Fresh Shelled Peas 69
    Vanilla Custard Ice Cream 69
    Jelly Cake 70
    Chocolate Pie, Meringue 71

Trinity: **The Scott Hotel** 73
  Recipes 80
    Pan-Fried Steak 80
    Cream Gravy 81
    Okra and Tomatoes 81
    Pear Preserves 82
    Vinegar Pie 83
    Baking Powder Biscuits 84
    Lye Soap 85

Kountze: **The Cariker Hotel** 87
  Recipes 91
    Chicken and Dumplings 91
    Spicy Roast 92
    Aunt Phein's Bread Pudding 93
    Lemon Sauce 93

Honey Island: **The Honey Island Boarding House** 95
  Recipes 101
    Pepper Relish 101
    Meat Loaf 102
    Spanish Rice 102
    Oatmeal Cookies 103
    Devil's Food Cake 104
    Seven-Minute Frosting 105
    Lemon Chess Pie 106
    Old-Fashioned Fudge 107

Colmesneil: **The East Texas Hotel** 109
  Recipes 113
    Chicken and Dressing 114
    Giblet Gravy 115
    Homemade Sausage 115

Country-Style Hominy 116
Fried Hominy 116
Sauerkraut 117
Southern Pecan Pie 118
Indian Pudding 119
Gingerbread with Raisin Cream Sauce 120
Sassafras Tea 121

Batson: The Caledonia/Aunt Doll's Boarding House . . 123
Recipes 131
  One-Two-Three-Four Cake 131
  Old-Fashioned Tea Cakes 132
  Fried Chicken 133
  Fried Frog Legs 134
  Creamed Stewed Onions 135
  Baked Sweet Potatoes 136
  Berry Cobbler 137

Saratoga: The Vines Hotel 139
Recipes 147
  Hog Killin' Day 147
  Preserving Pork 149
  Hog's Head Cheese 150
  Brains and Eggs 150
  Liver and Lights (Lungs) 151
  Fried Salt Pork 151
  Cracklings 151
  Crackling Corn Bread 152
  Crackling Hot Water Corn Bread 152
  Chitterlings (Chitlins) 153
  Fried Corn Pones 154
  Pigtails with Turnip Greens 154
  Pickled Pigs' Feet 154
  Special Vinegar Solution 155
  Fried Pigs' Feet 155

Bragg: The Bragg Hotel 157
  Recipes 164
    Old-Fashioned Meat Loaf 164
    Country Style Baked Fish 165
    Baked Deviled Eggplant Casserole 166
    Chili-Spaghetti Casserole 167
    Fresh Coconut Cake 168
    Coconut Frosting 168
    Sweet Potato Pie Deluxe 169
    Meringue 169
    Franklin Nut Cake 170
    Molasses Sugar Crisps 171
    Custard Fruit Cups 172
    Bread and Rice Pudding 173

Epilogue 174
Bibliography 177
Index 184

For my mother,
Minnie Burwick Crews,
Who knew the inns and out (houses)
of the Thicket.

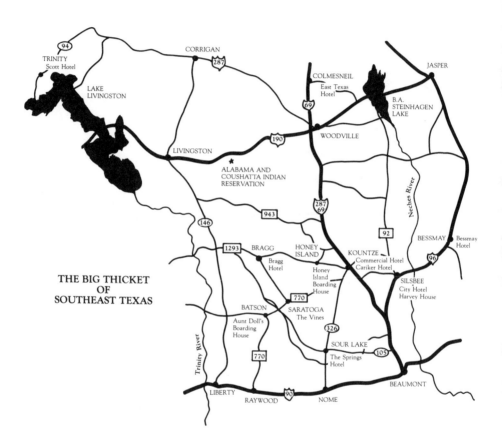

THE BIG THICKET
OF
SOUTHEAST TEXAS

**BIG THICKET
BOARDING HOUSES**

FOREWORD

Y ou don't usually think of boarding houses and recipes and eating when you think of the Big Thicket. You think of big woods with trees growing close together and straining to reach out of the brush to the sky and light above. You think of baygalls and damp spongy soil and palmettos rattling in the wind along edges of lazy gray bayous. If you are a naturalist your mind probably wanders back to Lance Rosier and pitcher plants and delicate white wild orchids. If you are a hunter you think of cat squirrels and wild hogs and a big buck easing out of the Thicket brush onto a logging road. Or, if you're a logger you might be thinking about how many Thicket trees you can cut before Timber Charlie and the big-city, tennis-shoed conservationists put the brakes on you. Point of view has a lot to do with one's perception of the Big Thicket.

And the point of view of this Big Thicket book by Wanda Landrey is the reminiscences and recipes of the boarding houses—the food and fixing it and eating it, and the stories of the people who ran them and stayed in them. This book is about the tales told by and about all of those folks in the boarding houses and the pork chops they served to the loggers, railroad hands, and roughnecks—and the mashed potatoes and gravy they served to the drummers and "ladies" that followed a boom, wherever it might occur—and the chicken and dumplings they served to all those who held together the Big Thicket social fabric during those boisterous, growing times.

When I'm wandering through the Thicket and eating crosses my mind—and it does every three or four hours—the first thing I think about is driving back to Kountze and the Top Half Cafe and getting on the outside of a chicken fried steak or a hamburger or a plate of scrambled eggs. And I'd say you can get to the Top Half in thirty minutes from just about anywhere in the Thicket, unless you're in the mud. When I'm on a hunt in the Thicket I usually carry a couple of fried pork chops and a peanut-butter-and-jelly sandwich, and that two-course meal tastes about as good as anything that Charles of the Ritz could whip up. And one time on Village Creek I paddled back into camp with a frazzling little string of bream that I gutted, scraped, and fried whole, and I do remember that at about two bites a fish that meal tasted as good as anything I ever bought at Catfish King. But as some would remind me, knowing my pecuniary disposition, they were free (unless you really started counting costs), and I was hungry enough to have eaten sweetgum bark if it had been battered and fried.

Those early settlers in the Thicket—the Collins, Overstreets, Hooks, Brackens, and their kin—didn't move to the Thicket because of its haute cuisine and five-star restaurants. But they soon saw that they had moved into a land of bears and honey, and they saw that they could eat regularly enough if they learned the land and what it could provide.

The food was there for the catching. The rivers and bayous and creeks had bream and bass and catfish—Ops and blues and channels—and washtub-size loggerhead turtles that would feed a family for days—and frog legs and alligator tails—and on up the bank and along the sloughs, crawfish for the seining.

Wild cattle—sprung from the loins of those that Cortéz brought into the New World at the city of the True Cross in 1519—grazed the coastal plains to the south of the Thicket. They came out at night, spooky as snakes, to graze the islands and prairies that were spotted through the Thicket. They were wild as the deer they grazed with, but the good woodsman could run them down and eat their meat and tan their hides. Wild hogs, the progeny of those that De Soto's expedition broadcast from Florida to East Texas roamed the woods as wary as bear and left their muddy marks where they rubbed the trees on their nightly forage. Beef and pork were food the Thicket settlers knew in both the wild and domesticated state.

Wood ducks nested during the summer along the bayous, and in the fall mallards and teal whistled into the flooded pin-oak flats to fatten on the acorns that made a bounty to every animal in the Thicket. In the winter on the coastal prairie below the Thicket, geese and ducks came in by the millions. They made many a good meal.

During most of the last century the big woods were not cut, except where families cleared a space for cabins and a corn patch and a vegetable garden close to the house. The Thicket was home for all sorts of good things to eat—squirrels, 'possums, and 'coons on a small scale and deer and bear as big game. Venison was a staple, and it was roasted or fried in bear fat or jerked and hung in the smoke house with the sausage and hams. Bear meat was a staple, but the great prize from a bear was the grease that was rendered and stored to cook with, because it stayed sweet and lasted longer than hog lard. And then most of the hogs were so lean that you couldn't wring a teacup of lard from a grown hog.

Beyond the game that the Lord provided if the hunter was a good shot, the woods furnished other foods—pecans, hickory nuts, and black walnuts—all of which were a lot of work for a little meat. Berries grew where a big wind laid down enough trees to let the sun reach the ground. 'Possum grapes grew along the creek banks, and muscadine vines climbed through the top branches to drop their grapes in the fall. And in the flats along the bayous mayhaws plopped their fruit in the rising waters, and if the fruit and water cooperated you could fill a washtub in an hour.

And in the spring the "denizens" (as Archer Fullingim of *The Kountze News* called them) drank sweet sassafras tea to thin their blood and ate poke salad to get iron back in their systems after a long, lean winter.

The Big Thicket was a good provider. Senator V. A. Collins—"Uncle Yank," as he was called—in 1962 told about his family living off the land in the previous century. Their only source of food was the wild hogs and game that his father Warren brought in. Deer were plentiful, he remembers, as were bear that fattened on the oak-tree mast. Uncle Yank, who was ninety-five during his reminiscence, remembered that his family ate well and that a log rolling was particularly festive: "The best food ever tasted was served; the most brilliant feast of the gods could not excel a log-rolling dinner." For Uncle Yank, eighty years away from that great spread, that was not hyperbole.

Outsiders didn't take to Thicket fare as well as Uncle Yank. A man by the name of George Caplen passed through the Thicket in 1887 and gave another view of eating in that area: "Their diet would by no means please the stomach of an epicure. Cornbread, bacon and potatoes, with an occasional treat of venison, gives them perfect satisfaction." At one stop Caplen's supper consisted of cornbread, very fat bacon, and clabber. He refused the clabber and could not get a cup of coffee to aid his digestive processes and suffered an excruciating headache as a result. Uncle Yank would have offered him little sympathy.

The primitive state of foodways ended in most parts of the Big Thicket in the 1880s. Logging companies and railroads came in and brought new people and new ways. And these new people — nomads, for the most part — had to have places to eat, thus the importance of the hotel and boarding house. After the turn of the century oil was discovered in the Thicket and more outsiders poured in to work on the rigs, and they all had to be fed.

The wanderers are gone now, or have settled and have their own table to sit down to, but the long board and the good foods and tales are still well remembered. The ideal fare in those booming days was food that would serve the field hand and still satisfy the gourmet. If you can't find the ideal among all the great recipes that Wanda Landrey collected in her Big Thicket ramblings, stop by the Top Half on your next Hardin County excursion. They still feed well in that part of the woods.

— *Francis Edward Abernethy*
Stephen F. Austin State University
Nacogdoches, Texas

ACKNOWLEDGEMENTS

S everal years ago my family and I more or less adopted an elderly widower into our fold, a man whom we called "Steph." Steph seemed to be lonely and we really enjoyed his company, so we got together with him whenever we could. An open invitation was extended for Sunday dinners, and sometimes he even went along on short weekend trips.

As a younger man Steph had worked as head of a large mule-skinning crew in Beaumont at Magnolia Refinery, now Mobil, in the days when mule-drawn wagons transported oil to various local destinations. He loved to reminisce about his days there, and since he was a great storyteller, we always listened intently. On one particular excursion with him, he made an analogy as we passed a Mobil service station. With his eyes twinkling, he looked up at the flying red horse on the sign in front of the station and said, "You know, Pegasus always got the credit, but the men and the mules did the work."

While writing this book, I often thought about Steph's statement and how actually nothing is unto itself. Certainly without the cooperation and enthusiasm exhibited by the scores of people interviewed, I wouldn't have had any stories to tell. I regret that I could not include them all, but, I hope the future holds another book. In addition to those interviewed, my job was made much easier by people such as David Payne of Sour Lake, Betty Mearns of Liberty, Inez Thornton of Chester, Nida Marshall of Jasper, James Read of Kountze, C. W.

Hendrix of Honey Island, Ruby Sutton of Port Neches, Thelma Hardy of Trinity, Thomasee Lewis of Saratoga, and Mable Bray of Beaumont. And as a history major who needed the help of some English majors to place commas, periods, and semi-colons in their proper places, very special thanks go to Beaumonters Gwen Beeson, Leah Rushing, and John Stansbury, each of whom not only assisted in editing at various stages but also gave me a lot of good ideas along the way. Last of all, Edna Hansford's skill and patience in typing and retyping the stories and recipes are sincerely appreciated. Indeed, no one goes his way alone.

PREFACE

G enerally speaking, Big Thicket boarding houses* came and went with the railroad, which was in its heyday from approximately the 1880s until the late 1930s. Although automobiles were coming into existence during the early years of the twentieth century, most Thicket roads were little more than dirt trails which were completely unreliable in bad weather. Passenger trains were more dependable but were still not guaranteed to arrive on time. Because of these precarious modes of travel, many eating and overnight lodging establishments were built, most within a stone's throw of the train depots.

For more than ten years I have traveled the highways and backroads in and beyond this land known as the Big Thicket of Texas, searching for people with stories about the old boarding houses. While I collected the stories, I also gathered old-time recipes along the way — and some photographs. The Big Thicket was fast disappearing and so was this colorful part of its culture. My goal was to save what remained of that interesting and colorful boarding house era so that future generations could read about it and enjoy it.

The Big Thicket, one of the most densely vegetated areas found anywhere in America, is sometimes referred to by scientists as the "Biological Cross-roads of North America" because of its unique and

---

* Many of the early Big Thicket boarding houses were called hotels, although they were in fact boarding houses where meals—or lodging and meals—could be bought. The terms "boarding house" and "hotel" are used interchangeably throughout this book.

diverse animal and plant life. Although it is difficult to determine where the region begins and ends, its general location is in the southeastern part of the state, north and northwest of the city of Beaumont. Spanning approximately fifty miles in length, it covers all of Hardin and parts of Liberty, Polk and Tyler counties. The Big Thicket means more to me than just an ecological anomaly. It is the land I love — the place where wonderful childhood memories exist, the home of my family who lived before me. My father's paternal grandparents settled in the Thicket in the 1840s when it was an unspoiled, almost impenetrable wilderness. Like so many other early American pioneers, my grandparents were an independent and self-reliant breed, who valued solitude more than close neighbors. They were among the first to invade the Thicket's interior, clearing small portions of it for their farmlands. The Thicket was their helpmate. What the settlers could not furnish for themselves, the land provided for them. They fished the creeks, bayous, and rivers; hunted the woods for wild game; and gathered a variety of nuts and fruits. They were the takers; the Thicket was the giver.

And as time went by, the people took more of the Thicket and took it faster. With the coming of the Industrial Revolution, railroads appeared, new towns came into being, and small communities grew. The forest, with its wealth of hardwoods and pines, proved a bonanza for many of the early timber barons who came and clear-cut vast sections of the land. The discovery of oil and the subsequent drilling brought about further desecration.

The people kept taking until finally someone realized that the Thicket soon would be able to give no more. Eventually, a concerted conservation battle was fought and won, and today a small portion of the land has been saved for posterity. The Big Thicket National Preserve, with its 84,550 acres, is a permanent reminder of the land of our ancestors.

Although some successful efforts have been made to save a part of the Thicket's unique environment, not enough has been done to preserve the ways and beliefs of its people and to capture the flavor of the early individualism which still exists among a few. Knowing I can make only a small ripple in the historical stream of the region's interesting culture, I have limited myself to the subject with which I am most familiar. Since I am a historian and a descendant of Big Thicket boarding house keepers, I have chosen to try to save that part of our Texas heritage.

I began my search at my father's old homeplace because I knew it held the key to the past. Once there, I was amazed at how alive my heritage became and how the picture of my objective focused. Suddenly, there was an urgency to find the survivors of that boarding house era while there was still a chance.

As I stood in my father's house that day, I could hear the low moaning whistle of a distant train. My mind flooded with a thousand happy memories of weekend rides on the Santa Fe "Doodlebug" from Beaumont to Kountze with my cousin Mary Ann. We had both felt grown-up as we hurried along the dusty roads leading from the depot to Grandpa's and Grandma's store, the Crews' Meat Market and Package Store. We looked forward to the adventures we knew we would have there, including socializing down at the store. We had been expressly forbidden to enter the side where Grandpa kept the liquor and for that reason felt compelled to do so, particularly since we could then indulge in one of our favorite pastimes—label-reading. Three Feathers, Old Grandad, and Four Roses were the ones which intrigued us most by conjuring up all sorts of interesting images in our minds. We also loved watching the occupants of the rocking chairs at the store and were able to pick up lots of valuable information that way, particularly from one frequent visitor—an old lady with a huge goiter that seemed to attract flies.

Before we could leave the store, we always had to check on the banana situation. Bananas were still a novelty item in Kountze then, and Grandpa usually had a stalk of them hanging in the front window to encourage people to come on in, which many did. Now, whenever I smell bananas, I'm reminded of those days.

Grandpa and Grandma Crews built a house when they were very young, soon after they came to Kountze in the early part of the century. They'd followed my grandmother's parents, Jim and Melissa Bradley,

Frank Crews in his general store (I don't think the woman
in the rocking chair is the one with the goiter!).
(*Courtesy Mrs. LaDonna Crews Schnick.*)

who had come to town earlier and had purchased the Commercial
Hotel.

With their move to that homeplace, Grandpa and Grandma Crews
established a tradition of love and laughter that lasted through their
seven children and continued until Grandpa's death in 1956. On the
day of his death, Grandma vowed that she would never spend another
night in the house—and she never did. Now the only resident is a
distant relative who takes care of what's left of my grandparents' hard
work and who keeps the contents undisturbed out of respect for the
family's wishes.

As I walked from room to room, each one was just as I remembered
it—only the furnishings are slowly and quietly aging with time. The

overstuffed sofa remains on the north wall of the living room, its cover more threadbare and faded than ever. And in the front bedroom, Grandma's most expensive material possession, a dark mahogany suite of furniture, still stands regally despite its cracked and dull finish. The pie safe in the dining room, a treasured inheritance from the old Commercial Hotel, looks as dismal as the old Lester piano in the corner.

I was delighted when my examination of the house turned up some old family pictures because they confirmed my suspicion that my family history was as vibrant as I had suspected. Rather than being the gloomy graveyard of lives and times gone by, it was instead a trove of tangible information about my heritage. About me. At that point, I had to know about more than just my grandparents; I wanted to know about my great-grandparents as well.

This old homeplace will always be an important link to the past for me. It was here the seeds of fascination for the past were originally planted in me, though by the time I could cultivate that interest in a more organized way, most of the principal participants were dead. The essence of the homeplace, which remains intact in my memory as well as in reality, generated the interest that resulted in this book.

Of all the steps it took to complete a history of Big Thicket boarding houses—researching old newspapers, magazines, and books, and testing the recipes—I enjoyed the personal interviews most. As a rule, almost all the people were eager to share their boarding house experiences with me. Oh, sometimes I had a little trouble, like the time I drove sixty miles to keep an appointment with a man whose wife wouldn't let him talk to me because she planned to write her own book and wanted to save the information for herself. And then there was the preacher who wanted a king's ransom for his treasured memories. However, as a result of approximately 140 interviews, I have developed a better understanding of Big Thicket boarding house living and rural life during this time in Texas.

This book is written not only to educate, but also to entertain and amuse. It is historically correct so far as possible, but considering that the stories are largely based on the memories of those who told them,

I imagine that some were embellished, while others omitted facts to create the proper story telling atmosphere.

The recipes presented here are some of the favorite taste treats of the period. Although today's cooks have access to so many more spices and convenience foods, these old-timey foods are hard to beat. Of course, many of the earlier recipes were never written down and subsequently may have gotten garbled through their oral transmissions. Because I wanted them to be as authentic as possible, I not only checked with several older cooks but also tested, tasted, and retested the majority of them myself. They taste just right.

I've loved this project and will always be grateful to all the folks who shared their reminiscences and recipes with me.

— *Wanda A. Landrey*

Wanda Crews in Grandma's garden.

The Bradley women in front of the Commercial Hotel. *Seated:* Mittye,
Melissa. *Standing:* Ila, Cora Crews and three daughters.
(Photograph found in an old trunk at the Crews homeplace.)

The Commercial Hotel

I f the word "lagniappe" had been in vogue during the early twentieth century in the Big Thicket, it would have perfectly described the accommodations at the Commercial Hotel, one of the most popular boarding establishments in the area. It really did offer "that something extra."

The hotel was an imposing two-story structure, looking majestic and almost out-of-place along the railroad tracks and narrow main road that led from the depot to the courthouse. Cleanliness, meaning no bedbugs; progressiveness, including a carbide light system; and good food were foremost among the amenities desired by travelers. Of course, these early niceties would seem primitive in comparison to today's standards, but they were quite luxurious for the time—enough so that guests paid twice the going rate—two dollars a day!

Nobody's quite sure when the hotel was built, but it was relatively new when my great-grandparents, Jim and Melissa Bradley and their three young children, Mittye, Ila, and Barney, moved to Kountze in 1900 to become its new owners. The opportunity to buy the hotel arose after the Reddings, the original owners, died of a mysterious lung disease, a malady which ended the lives of all six members of the family.

When the Bradleys arrived, Kountze was only a one-horse town, but since they'd come from the no-horse sawmill community of Mobile, near the town of Woodville, it seemed like big-time progress to them. Actually, their expectations for economic success were well-founded. Not only was Kountze the county seat of Hardin County, but it was also the junction of two railroads, the T&NO (Texas and New Orleans) and the Santa Fe.

Trains, still in their infancy in Southeast Texas, often went at a turtle's pace, but when they did deposit a passenger at the depot, the visitor was sure to be interesting. For the first time, area folks were coming face-to-face with persons of other cultural backgrounds and beliefs.

Fortunately, the railroad schedules boosted the hotel business because even straight connections were hard to make, and relatively short trips, such as from Woodville to Kountze, required an over-night stay in Kountze. Whether the travelers were going to be in town for a few hours or a few days, the conveniently located hotel could accommodate them.

Some of the most exciting guests who stayed at the Commercial were the distant hunters from the North and Northeast who periodically converged on the Big Thicket in search of the highly-prized black bear. It was the custom around the turn of the century for groups of them to spend the night there before proceeding to the Hooks' Camp near the oil field town of Saratoga. Indeed, their tales of adventure must have been intriguing to the Thicket folks who rarely ventured more than thirty miles from home.

In addition to the hunters came the traveling salesmen, or drummers, as they were called then. At least three times a year, droves of dry-goods salesmen descended on the area from the big marketing capitals of St. Louis, Chicago, Houston, Galveston, and New Orleans. To accommodate the drummers, the Bradleys built a big showroom adjacent to the hotel. It served as a miniature market center where the salesmen could show off their wares to the merchants of the surrounding areas. The merchants, of course, also stayed at the hotel.

A drill group in front of the Commercial Hotel—School program, 1906.
Some of the girls identified: Kate Vickers, Anna Vickers, Bertha Vickers,
Ruby Herrington, Ila Bradley, Mary Ella Yankie, and Ola Brakin.
(*Courtesy Mrs. Minnie McKim.*)

My great-aunt Ila, the younger of the Bradley girls, told me that
the women in her family always looked forward to market time because
they loved to see the trunks of beautiful clothes.

> The drummers would stay here for a week at a time, sometimes two
> weeks. The merchants had to make reservations because so many people
> came, even merchants from Beaumont. They'd come in the spring, the
> late summer, and the fall for Christmas-time.
>
> Papa operated the showroom until 1910, the year that Halley's comet
> appeared in the sky. One night, we had a big storm, and it ripped the
> roof off the room and blew parts of it over to the Negro quarters. The
> next morning, everybody got really excited because they throught they
> were pieces from the comet. After that, the sample room was turned
> into a skating rink.

Other noteworthy gatherings at the hotel occurred when court was
in session, generally twice a year. It was then that the circuit judge

and jurors, as well as a host of curious spectators, stayed there. One of the most memorable times was when the Sapp *habeas corpus* hearing was held in 1915. This hearing created interest throughout the state after a series of murders occurred in the Big Thicket involving two well-known Beaumonters, Emory Eran Sapp and his younger half-brother, Louis Sapp. The *habeas corpus* hearing was held to show cause why the defendants should not be released on bail. * For this hearing, people flocked to Kountze from all over the area, and as a result, the hotel did a land-office business. There were so many guests, in fact, that it was necessary to spread pallets in the halls as well as out on the porches.

Although Grandpa Bradley had been physically disabled as a result of a logging accident, his family was by no means emotionally or monetarily disabled because of his handicap. He met every train that came to town. If travelers wanted lodging at the Commercial, he was happy to oblige them. If they wanted to stay somewhere else, why, his livery stable would provide them with round-trip transportation. After all, he was flexible, for a reasonable fee. In addition to assisting Grandma at the hotel, he grew vegetables which he conveniently sold to her for the hotel kitchen. I never could understand just exactly how Grandpa Bradley could bring himself to charge his own wife for food that he was going to actually eat later. But, since he was her sidekick most of the time, it probably did make him feel better to have a few coins of his own jingling in his pockets.

Grandpa Bradley's concern for money became so apparent that his own small grandchildren picked up on it and decided to play a trick on him. Grandpa had a watermelon patch. One day, when he was taking a nap, my dad and his sisters entered Grandpa's forbidden watermelon patch, broke open the biggest melons, and ate only the hearts. Careful to destroy any tell-tale evidence, they carried off what was left, buried it, and painstakingly brushed away their footprints. Grandpa was outraged, but fortunately for the children, he never did figure out who did the mischievous deed.

---

*Events leading to the murders and the solution of the crimes formed an almost unbelievable story. For more information, consult my book, *Outlaws in the Big Thicket*, 1976, Austin, Eakin Publications.

But Grandpa Bradley could get more than just blood out of turnips! He realized that there was value in another one of his commodities as well—his beautiful daughter, Mittye. Although Aunt Hettie, my dad's oldest sister, was a young girl at the time, she was old enough to be impressed by her fashionable Aunt Mittye, and remembered that "She was pretty as a picture and stayed primped all the time. That face was fixed, that hair was combed, those nails were painted. Auntie's job was to register the guests and play dominos and cards with the drummers that came through."

Mittye was such a hit with everybody that Grandpa discouraged anyone other than paying guests from hanging around the hotel trying to monopolize her time. His tactics were not tactful, but they were successful. He would first tell her young suitors to hit the dusty trail. Then, if that did not work, he would slip them a note. Nobody seemed to know what his messages said, but apparently they were forceful. Before long, the young boys stopped coming . . . and Mittye never did get married.

Unfortunately, the more money Grandpa made the grumpier he got until Grandma finally packed his bags and shuffled him upstairs to stay by himself in a lonely cubicle until his disposition improved. He never did get to move back down. As usual, money alone was not enough to bring happiness!

You would have thought that Grandpa Bradley would have learned that money was not the answer to his problems. He had not learned at all, and in 1916 he began looking restlessly around for greener pastures. When he thought he had found them, he sold the hotel to the Norton family and he and his family moved to the wild oil fields of Saratoga to operate the Rio Bravo Boarding House. The Commercial Hotel operated until 1925 when it burned to the ground in less than forty-five minutes. A bucket brigade of volunteer firemen was no match for a fire out of control. Although another hotel was soon built on the site, it never did equal the success of the original Commercial, and several years later, the building was sold to the Williford family for a general merchandise store.

COMMERCIAL HOTEL RECIPES

 CHICKEN POT PIE

Melissa Bradley, like most other Thicket innkeepers, didn't need a course in bookkeeping to learn to balance her budget. She simply prepared the best food she could for the least amount of money. Chicken, the cheapest and most available meat around, was prepared often and in a variety of ways to make the meals interesting.

> 1 medium chicken
> salt and pepper to taste
> 1 cup chopped onions
> 1 cup sliced carrots
> 1 cup sifted flour
> ½ teaspoon salt
> 1 teaspoon baking powder
> cream

Place the seasoned chicken in a large pot, adding enough water to cover. Bring to a boil. Cover, reduce the heat, and simmer the chicken until tender. Remove the chicken from the broth and cool. Bone the chicken, cut the meat into pieces, and set aside. Heat approximately 3 cups of the chicken broth in a pan with enough flour to make a gravy. If desired, season more with salt and pepper. Set aside. Cook the vegetables in a small amount of boiling, salted water until tender. Drain. Put the vegetables and the chicken pieces in a casserole dish and cover with the gravy.

Sift flour, salt, and baking powder together into a bowl. Add enough cream to make a soft dough. Roll on a floured board. Cut into small biscuits. Place biscuits on top of the casserole mixture and bake at 400° until biscuits are brown.

SWEET POTATO CASSEROLE

No Thanksgiving dinner was complete at the Commercial without this special dish, and it's been a tradition in our family ever since. (The bourbon was later added by my mother to give it a little zing-g-g.)

    5 large sweet potatoes
    6 tablespoons butter
    ½ to ¾ cup canned milk
    2 eggs
    1½ cups brown sugar
    2 cups marshmallows, cut up (They didn't have
        miniature marshmallows back then.)
    1 teaspoon vanilla extract
    1 teaspoon cinnamon
    1 teaspoon nutmeg
    1 cup chopped pecans
    ½ cup bourbon
    marshmallows (for topping)

Gently boil sweet potatoes until tender. Peel the hot potatoes and mash. Melt the butter and, along with the milk and the eggs, add to the potatoes. Beat until fluffy. Stir in the other ingredients, reserving the large marshmallows. Pour into a 2-quart casserole. Top with marshmallows and bake at 350° until marshmallows brown.

 JAM CAKE

During the early days, resourceful cooks lined their pantry shelves with a variety of canned fruits and vegetables. One of the most popular fruit preserves was blackberry jam because of the abundance of the wild blackberries which grew in the area. It was used as a delicious condiment for hot breads and as an important ingredient in this spicy cake.

Batter:

> ¾ cup butter
> 1½ cups sugar
> 4 egg yolks
> 1 cup blackberry jam
> 3 cups flour
> ½ teaspoon salt
> 1 teaspoon cinnamon
> 1 teaspoon nutmeg
> 1 teaspoon cloves
> 1 teaspoon baking soda
> ¾ cup buttermilk
> 4 egg whites, beaten until frothy

Cream butter with sugar. Add the egg yolks, one at a time, beating well. Stir in blackberry jam. Sift flour with salt and spices. Stir soda into buttermilk. Add flour and buttermilk mixtures alternately to creamed mixture, stirring well. Fold in egg whites. Turn into three greased and floured 9-inch layer pans. Bake at 350° until done.

Filling:

> 3 tablespoons flour
> 1 cup sugar
> 2 eggs
> 1 cup milk
> lump of butter

Cook ingredients in a double boiler and stir until mixture is thick enough to spread between layers.

Icing:
>   3 cups sugar
>   1 cup butter
>   1½ cups canned milk
>   1 teaspoon vanilla

Place sugar, butter, and milk into a pan and bring to a boil. Boil mixture until it makes a soft ball in water. Beat until thick. Add vanilla. Cool. Spread over the cake top and sides.

EGG CUSTARD PIE

>   3 eggs, well beaten
>   1 cup sugar
>   2 tablespoons flour
>   1 small can evaporated milk
>   1¼ cups sweet milk
>   butter
>   nutmeg

Cream eggs and sugar well. Stir in flour, evaporated milk, and sweet milk. Pour mixture into unbaked 8-inch pie shell. (See East Texas Hotel recipes, page 118, for pie crust recipe.) Dot pie with bits of butter, sprinkle with nutmeg, and bake at 350° for 25 minutes or until set.

RED-EYE GRAVY

According to George Leonard and Bertha E. Herter's *Bull Cook and Authentic Historical Recipes*, red-eye gravy, an old Southern favorite, got its name from General Andrew Jackson, the seventh President of the United States. One day, while Old Hickory was still a general, he sat down to have his noon meal and called his cook over to tell him what to prepare. The cook had been drinking white mule (Southern moonshine corn whiskey) the night before, and his eyes were as red as fire. General Jackson, never a man to mince words, told the cook to bring him some country ham with gravy as red as his eyes. Some men nearby heard the general, and ham gravy became red-eye gravy from that day on.

Take a large frying pan, put a heaping tablespoon of lard into the pan, and melt it. When melted, put in slices of ham and fry them until well done. Add 1 cup of water and 1 crushed clove. Bring to a boil and simmer for 5 minutes. Remove the ham and serve some gravy with the ham.

Red-eye gravy also tastes good when served over grits.

 BEEF TEA

Grandma Bradley was well-known for her kindness to scores of down-and-out folks who came her way. She had a special recipe for beef tea, or extracta, that was guaranteed to help anybody feel better, no matter how serious the ailment. In fact, if she got there in time, even death-bed confessions sometimes had to be postponed because of the miraculous recovery of the sick. Ruby Herrington, who gave me Grandma's recipe, told me that her father had actually been saved by Grandma Bradley's beef tea.

She would select a good lean piece of beef, put it into a jar without water, and seal the jar. She would then place the sealed container in a pot of boiling water and cook the meat until most of the juice had been extracted.

I tried this using a shank cross-cut of beef and observed that it does taste a lot better than the beef bouillon available today.

Springs Hotel, Sour Lake, Texas.

SOUR LAKE

THE SPRINGS HOTEL RESORT

I n the 1880s the Springs, a health spa in what is now the town of Sour Lake, was at its height. Its buildings included a luxurious colonial-style hotel nestled in the shadows of huge moss-draped oaks, bathhouses at the edge of a sparkling lake fed by several mineral springs, and a pavilion in the middle of the lake connected to the shore by an ornamental footbridge. This tranquil setting at the southeastern edge of the Big Thicket helped make it one of the most frequently patronized health resorts in the South.

Long before the white man touted the powers of the medicinal water, Indians had known of its secrets. Legend has it that coastal Indians, living near the present town of High Island, were the first to discover the springs after a plague swept their village, threatening to wipe out their entire number. One day the chief's beautiful daughter died, and the medicine men were powerless. That night the girl appeared before her father in a vision and promised him that she would come back to earth in another form and lead her people to a magic lake fed by many springs where they could drink, bathe, and recover.

The next morning a lovely white doe appeared, and the chief instantly knew that it was the reincarnated spirit of his beloved daughter.

The first Sour Lake Springs Hotel? Although this picture has been labeled
the Sour Lake Hotel, many local sources believe the building to be another
facility used by hotel guests. *(Courtesy Big Thicket Museum.)*

Led by the doe, the remaining tribal members formed a slow procession
and eventually came to the promised water. Soon after the ailing
entourage arrived, the white doe disappeared into the forest, never to
be seen again; the Indians drank from the springs, bathed in the lake,
and soon recovered.

More factual than the "white doe" Indian story are accounts of
wandering tribes from as far away as Mexico and Louisiana who knew
of the healing powers of the sour springs and visited often. Since no
trace of weapons has ever been found in the area, it is believed that
the Indians always observed some form of truce there.

In 1834 the first title of ownership of the springs went to Stephen
Jackson, when the Mexican government granted him one thousand
acres of land in Southeast Texas. It is said that Jackson and some of

The second Springs Hotel as it appeared in the 1880s. (The hotel was completed in March, 1882, and burned on March 21, 1909. Sour Lake resident Anna Mae Hardage said that her mother, Alice Cotton, would go to dances called "Germans" at the hotel. "The young folks would go at midnight and dance until dawn. They put on their best 'bibs and tuckers' and went to the ball.") *(Courtesy Ray Edmondson.)*

his men rode out on the range one day and, spotting the lake, decided to drink from it. Jackson was the first to dismount and drink. One swallow of the bitter water was all it took to convince Jackson that he surely would die. But die he didn't, and soon he began actually to feel better. From then on, the news of his discovery traveled, and by 1845 the reputation of the healing waters was well established.

The resort died a quick death in 1909 when its second hotel burned, and few area residents remembered anything more than handed-down stories about the spa era. Eda Belle Boyd, a resident of Daisetta, spent her childhood years in Sour Lake. As a small girl, Eda Belle lived near the Springs and was so impressed by the magnitude of the hotel and the frilly clothes worn by the lady guests that she remembered a great deal about the early days of the spa.

> The hotel seemed like a huge thing to me because we lived in what we called a shotgun house. We were poor kids who lived in the oil field, so of course I was fascinated by what was goin' on over there. The hotel had a long porch in front where the people would sit in rockin' chairs. The guests came from everywhere, you know, even big cities up North . . . . In the real early days they would come by train to Nome* and then take a hack the six miles or so to Sour Lake. They came to take the baths in the lake there, you know, for arthritis. . . . They didn't call it that then; they called it rheumatism. . . . This lake, it had sulphur mud that they were puttin' on 'em. In the evening after the baths, they'd get all dressed up and paddle around the lake. The women would have a parasol over 'em to keep from gettin' sunburned. I can remember that well because I never had anything with that embroidery, you know, ruffles on the bottom.

Additional clues to the daily activities at the Springs were found in several early area newspapers. One descriptive account, written by a reporter who just had returned from a visit there, appeared in the *Galveston Daily News* on August 28, 1883.

> I am back from a visit to Sour Lake. . . . I left Galveston some two weeks ago, worn, weak, and languid, with barely enough energy left to rise in the morning and retire at night. I found at Sour Lake about 120 visitors, chiefly from Texas and Louisiana. The old hotel and cottages have disappeared; new and better buildings have taken their place, but the lake and wells are still there—the greatest wonder in all nature that this country has ever furnished.

---

*One undocumented source tells that when railroad passengers arrived at the depot in Nome, they often asked the agent if they were in Sour Lake. "Nome," he would answer, meaning "No Ma'am." Of course, the people didn't know that, and they started calling the place Nome.

Ready for a hunt at the Springs Resort Stables.
(*Courtesy Ray Edmondson.*)

Leaving Galveston at 3:30 p.m., we reached the lake about 10 o'clock that night. The buildings and grounds were lighted up, music and dancing was making happy the young who had gathered in the parlor . . . . The first I recognized was Mrs. P. J. Willis, wife of the owner. . .

I found the old and the young suffering from rheumatism, disepsia [sic], indigestion, paralysis, nervous prostration, and every character almost of cutaneous diseases. One day at the lake arms us with a ravenous appetite. . . We had an abundance of good substantial food. . . . The great leading feature which I found in the lake was the mud bath. This consists of a plunge in the water to open the pores of the skin, then plastering the body from the crown of head to the soles of the feet with mud taken from the bottom of the lake, and permitting this coat to remain on the person from ten to twenty-five minutes . . . then another plunge in the water, and five minutes there getting rid of the mud, then two buckets of water poured on top of your head, or as "Dr. Paul," the clever attendant calls it, a "send-off," then the vigorous application of a crash towel, and you go out all aglow, feeling "like a strong man [about] to run a race."

There are ten wells and four pools from which we drink the waters, all near each other, but differing widely in taste and appearance — all strongly impregnated with minerals, chief among which are sulphur, alum, and iron, though the great drawbacks to the use of these waters is the fact that no analysis has ever been made of them.

One of the most popular employees at the Springs in the late 1800s was a black man named Brazile. It is said that before coming to the resort, Brazile had acquired knowledge of the healing powers of the water and mud and, as a result, had established himself as a kind of medicine man among the blacks. At the Springs, his expertise at massages and effective applications of mud packs earned him the prestigious title of "Dr. Mud."

Dr. Mud must have been an interesting looking figure while scurrying among the guests at the lake. Described as tall and thin, Dr. Mud had a long beard and dressed in a white top hat, one of many campaign hats worn during Grover Cleveland's race for President of the United States. Along with the hat, he wore a long-tailed coat and dress pants, both too short for his gangly frame.

He may have been comical in appearance, but he was obviously no dunce when it came to appealing to a woman's ego. For the lady, his beauty treatment consisted of a mud mask, which was applied to the face at night and left on until morning, and a prescription of fine light-colored soil, which was used as a face powder.

One story depicting Dr. Mud's diplomacy when administering to the ladies who came to the Springs told about how he handled three rather homely ladies who just had arrived from New Orleans. Recognizing him from descriptions they had heard, the women walked over to him and one of them asked if he could prescribe some beauty treatment. Dr. Mud studied each woman for a moment and then answered, "Yes, Ma'am, I'll give you some nice beauty mud, but I don't think you needs it."

When the hotel burned in 1909, the glamour of the era was over. Dr. Mud was dead by then and the rush for oil quickly changed the population of Sour Lake from less than one thousand to over ten thousand. The new breed of twentieth-century opportunists and investors, who had replaced the nineteenth-century genteel folks, obviously were interested more in black gold than therapeutic mud. The boomers came and went, however, and in the late '20s serious plans were made by local businessmen to rebuild the Springs resort. Unfortunately, the stock market crash of 1929 ended their dreams, and, as far as can be determined, no other action was ever taken.

I must admit that while I found the stories of the Sour Lake spa interesting, I still was perplexed over the actual benefits that patients received there. It is true that the reporter who visited the Springs in 1883 said he felt better, but he wrote his article only three days after his return. He still could have been experiencing a sense of euphoria that often accompanies traveling. The only other testimony that I read came from Sam Houston's visit to the Springs in May, 1863, when he was treated for some old battle wounds. Houston may have found relief from his pain while staying there, but his overall health obviously did not improve; several months later he died at his home in Huntsville.

Finally, I came across an unidentified article in my files entitled, "Sour Lake, Texas: Health Resort of the Nineteenth Century." The paper, written probably in the 1960s, contained a personal interview with Dr. John M. Montgomery, the only practicing physician in Sour Lake at that time. Dr. Montgomery actually had treated some of the old-timers of the area who earlier had visited the old springs for relief from arthritis. According to him, there was no healing power in the mud and water. The mud packs may have temporarily eased the arthritic pain, but they didn't cure the illness. Dr. Montgomery thought the most beneficial physical result was that the sulfuric compounds in the water caused the patient's bowels to move; as a result, the patient's mental attitude brightened because he believed he had improved physically.

David Payne, a resident of Sour Lake, examines pilings at the edge of the old Springs Resort lake. Today the lake and its mineral springs are dry.

Even if the spa didn't offer relief from illness, it must have been great fun to wallow around in all the mud and joke with Dr. Mud in the morning; get dressed up in the afternoon, complete with pantaloons and parasol, and have some fancy dandy row you around the lake; then, at night dance in the ballroom of the big hotel and enjoy lively conversation on the front porch.

THE SPRINGS HOTEL RESORT RECIPES

Searching for special old recipes often can be like looking for a needle in a haystack, especially when hunting back as far as the nineteenth-century Springs Hotel. There, even the haystack was elusive! And since the lake and its acidic springs are dried up now, there's not even enough mud to mix a pie or water to make lemonade.

However, clues to the type of food served at the resort still do exist. In a flowery account which appeared in the *Galveston Daily News* on July 14, 1857, a reporter showed that the management at the Springs was interested in whole body fitness, a concept familiar to most of us today:

> Besides the benefit to be derived from the use of the waters, there is a delightful and healthful climate . . . cool and bracing breezes constantly blowing from the Gulf . . . prairies and forests abundantly stocked with every description of wild game, affording exercise and rare sport to such as are fond of it, and excellent food for stomachs disgusted with the spiced and 'doctored' diet of the cities. . . .

Although selected diets were prescribed by a Dr. Richardson for "the man with the torpid liver . . . he of the rheumatic joints," the writer of the article observed that many of the patients chose to "defy the healing power of the waters and continue the process of slow and certain suicide, by the use of coffee, tea, hot biscuit and the castor's contents."

While the writer apologized for his medical lecture, he further advised guests to

> exercise that most difficult of all christian [sic] virtues, self-denial, and choose water or milk for his beverage, and the plain

cold wheat bread, the corn bread, fresh eggs, the chicken, venison,
beef, or squirrel meat, the boiled rice, and the potatoes, for his diet. . . .

Sour Lake resident Jessie Lea Mowbray told me that her father,
Preston Mowbray, was an avid hunter in the late 1800s and supplied
the Springs with most of its wild game. "Once," said Jessie, "my father
killed enough ducks and geese to make five feather mattresses. At that
time a lot of people in a small community cooked alike," Jessie continued. "It was the way one was taught—by word of mouth. "

Since wild game hunters are often the best wild game cooks, the
following recipes, which were Preston Mowbray's favorites, may have
been used at the Springs.

    PAN-FRIED VENISON

1 venison backstrap
minced garlic to taste
salt and pepper to taste
egg, milk and flour batter
¾ cup shortening

Slice the backstrap thin and rub each slice with minced garlic. Beat
on both sides to tenderize. Season generously with salt and pepper.
Dip in well-beaten egg and milk batter, then in flour. Melt the
shortening in an iron skillet and fry floured meat rapidly over high
heat, turning once, until browned on both sides. Make gravy from
the pan drippings.

   DRIED VENISON

Cut venison into chunks. Mix 2 cups coarse salt, ½ cup coarse ground
pepper, and 2 teaspoons saltpeter. Rub chunks with seasonings and
put in a crock bowl. Let stand at least 24 hours. String each chunk
and dip in boiling water until meat turns white. Hang up and smoke.
When dry, venison is ready to serve.

VENISON ROAST

Season roast with salt and pepper, rubbing well into surface of meat, and sear in hot bacon drippings in heavy pot until brown all over. Place meat in a roasting pan without a rack and lay a large bacon rind over it. Cover and roast at 325° to 350° from 3 to 4 hours, depending on the size of the roast. Add water if no liquid forms in your roaster after a short time. If desired, add carrots and onions to the drippings. Baste occasionally.

 ## VENISON CHILI

Use meat from neck, ribs and shoulders, trimming off fat. Cut meat in small chunks. Measure 1 ½ tablespoons chili powder for each pound of meat and add to meat. Add salt and pepper to taste. Set meat aside.

Use 4 dried, red chili pods for each pound of meat. Remove stems and seeds and wash. Boil until tender. Remove pods from water and reserve water. Peel and mince pods and add to meat. Set aside.

Use one-fourth as much tallow (preferably beef tallow) as venison and cut into chunks. Put part of cut-up tallow in heavy pan and melt. Add minced garlic pods (1 for each pound of venison) to melted tallow and cook until lightly browned. Mix remainder of tallow with seasoned venison, add to pan, and cook until meat turns white. Add just enough water to cover, using water retained from boiling chili pods also. Lower temperature and continue cooking, adding more water if needed.

 **SQUIRREL STEW**

2 or 3 squirrels, quartered
salt and pepper to taste
3 tablespoons flour
3 tablespoons shortening
2 large onions, chopped
2 cups water
3 potatoes, peeled and cubed
4 carrots, peeled and sliced

Salt and pepper squirrels. Roll in flour. Melt shortening in a Dutch oven. Brown squirrels in hot oil. Remove squirrels and add 3 tablespoons flour to the oil, stirring until brown. Sauté the onions in the flour mixture until wilted. Add water and stir. Return squirrels to the pot and cook over low heat about 1 hour or until tender. Add vegetables and cook for 15 minutes, or until the potatoes are done.

SQUIRREL AND DUMPLINGS

2 squirrels
1 cup buttermilk
¼ teaspoon baking powder
2 tablespoons shortening, melted
1 teaspoon salt
1⅔ cups flour
butter
pepper

Boil squirrels in salted water until the meat falls off the bone. Discard bones. Set meat aside and reserve broth. Mix buttermilk, baking powder, melted shortening, salt, and enough flour to make a stiff dough. Roll paper thin and cut in small strips. Put meat back in pot of broth and bring to a rolling boil. Drop dumplings in, one at a time, adding dots of butter and pepper. Lower temperature, cover pot, and simmer for 15 to 20 minutes.

ROAST DUCK, SQUIRREL, OR GOOSE

Rub meat generously with salt and pepper. Cut small slits over surface of meat and insert each slit with a small piece of garlic and a small pod of red pepper. Fill cavity of each animal with slices of an apple to help remove "gamey" taste.

Pour a small amount of bacon drippings into a roasting pan and heat in a hot oven. Place seasoned meat in pan and brown all over, turning often. After browning, reduce oven to a moderately low temperature, add a small amount of water, cover pan, and continue cooking until meat is tender. While cooking, add water as needed and turn meat often. Serve along with drippings for gravy.

BEAR MEAT

Bear meat from the Thicket, especially from an old bruin, was tough and required special treatment in its preparation. To tenderize the meat before cooking, it had to be well-seasoned with salt and pepper and boiled in water or soaked in a marinade for at least 24 hours.

Marinade (for a 6 lb. roast)
>   2 cups water
>   1 cup vinegar
>   ½ cup olive oil
>   2 bay leaves
>   ½ teaspoon sage
>   ¼ teaspoon allspice
>   6 cloves
>   ¼ teaspoon nutmeg
>   ½ teaspoon red pepper
>   ½ teaspoon garlic, minced
>   2 tablespoons chopped onions

Boil all ingredients 3 minutes then cool to room temperature before placing meat in the marinade.

Remove meat from marinade. Season with salt and pepper. Place meat in roaster and cover with 2 sliced onions. Cover roasting pan and bake in a slow oven (30 minutes per lb.). Add water if necessary.

The Badders Hotel around 1906. (*Courtesy May Overland.*)

THE BADDERS HOTEL/
THE CITY HOTEL

J ohn Henry Kirby, an East Texas timber baron, was a man of vision who realized one very important principle of success: to be able to achieve something in reality, you must first be able to achieve it in your dreams. He was able to succeed at the turn of the century when others weren't because of his incredible ability to sell his dreams of a vast forest empire to wealthy financiers from the North. They were intrigued by the promises of the persuasive Kirby that trees were as good as, if not actually better than, gold. After all, the piney woods could naturally renew themselves in a relatively short time, but once mined, gold was gone forever.

One of his main backers was Nathaniel Silsbee, a Boston attorney, who was honored in 1894 by having the townsite of Kirby's first mill named after him. The Texas entrepreneur must have believed that he could not fulfill his ambitious goals for Silsbee if he began with a shoddy operation, because in addition to his first-class mill, Kirby built a large commissary, about 100 above-average company houses, several fine homes in which his relatives could wine and dine his potential investors, and two nice hotels—the Kirby Mill Hotel and the Badders, later called the City Hotel. With the exception of the house occupied

Eugenia Nixson.
(*Courtesy Eugenia
Nixson.*)

by Attorney Houston Thompson, former home of Kirby's brother Jim,
who was an early mill manager—and a few smaller structures, the
original Kirby buildings have disappeared. Only recently, the City
Hotel, built by Kirby in the section of town called Junction close to
the Santa Fe Railroad, was demolished.

The last person to live in the dilapidated City Hotel was Mrs.
Eugenia Nixson, who had operated the business since 1944. I first
visited Mrs. Nixson there in the winter of 1981, and I can remember
the weather outside matched the inside of the building—dark and
gloomy. Although the environment was chilly in every way, my spirits

were lifted by the warmth of Mrs. Nixson, who assured me that she would help me trace the history of the place back to its beginning in 1902. She referred me to two area residents, Mrs. May Overland and Mr. A. S. Norrid, who had both grown up in the hotel.

When I first met May Overland, I couldn't help but think of one of my favorite poems, "When I Am An Old Woman" by Elizabeth Lucas. May, like the elderly woman in the poem, had reached that delightful stage in life when one adopts the philosophy that it's okay to "wear purple with a red hat . . . sit down when I'm tired . . . and make up for the sobriety of my youth . . . go out in slippers in the rain . . . and learn to spit." May Overland was much too dignified to spit, but she wasn't about to take life too seriously either, and I always found her to be delightfully entertaining. The flame deep within this lovely lady may have changed from a fast-burning blue to a mellower yellow, but the sparks in her heart could still ignite as she relived the exciting times of her youth.

May's mother was Mary Elizabeth Clark Badders, one of the first managers of the hotel. May wasn't sure just why her parents moved to Silsbee, but she did know that her father, William James Badders, and John Henry Kirby "were the best of friends." During the family's first few years there, her father was an officer of the law, and her mother ran the Badders Hotel with both jobs generating excitement for everybody.

Her father often got called out in the middle of the night to make an arrest. Since there wasn't a jail in town, he would just take his prisoner to the hotel and chain him to one of his sons' beds. The next day, he would haul the prisoner to the county jail in Kountze. Growing boys need lots of sleep, and this process wasn't very conducive to their getting it. Fortunately, though, a sub-jail called a calaboose was finally built in Silsbee, and so May's brothers were able to rest much better after that.

John Henry Kirby always tried to fill key positions with his relatives, but sometimes that did not work. He had originally had his nephew running his Junction hotel, but, like so many cases of nepotism, this one also fizzled out in failure. Kirby then recruited May's mother as manager, knowing that she was a reliable individual and a great cook.

He especially loved her fruitcakes and would always ask her to make some for Christmas.

For May, there was never a dull moment at the hotel during those early years. The only girl in the family, she had three older and three younger brothers, who quickly taught her the principles involved in the game of survival of the fittest. "They would torture me by putting lizards on me and would play so many tricks that I was afraid to even go out on the porch at night. The only way that I could protect myself was to throw things at them—hammers, butcher knives, anything I could get my hands on . . . and I really aimed to hit 'em, too."

If cooking, housekeeping chores, and refereeing her lively children's battles were not enough to keep Mrs. Badders busy, surely the unruly behavior of some of her boarders was. According to May, her mother was never a person who shirked her responsibilities, and one of her biggest jobs was to try to keep peace in the hotel at night.

Back in those days, nobody had locks on doors because nobody stole or nothing. Anyway, one night this drunk stumbled into this woman's room and got in bed with her while she was sleeping—dirty clothes and all. After awhile, the woman woke up and started screaming and hollering. It wasn't anytime before Mother went up there, and she pulled off her shoes, and she whacked him on the head all the way down the steps.

We had crooked women who stayed there from time to time . . . . One of them stayed in a room upstairs right next to a telegraph operator and his wife who was a little deaf. One morning, the wife came down and said, "Miz Badders, that woman over there is crooked . . . and she got my husband out of bed last night." Well, Mother marched right over there and told her that crooked or not, if she planned to stay there any longer, she'd better straighten up quick or hit the road. The woman just looked at her and laughed, but she did pack up and leave that day.

Everytime there was a crooked woman in the hotel, it was guaranteed that Mr. _____ or Mr. _____ would show up. When they did, Mother would say, "Well, I got a whore in the house tonight. I'll have to check this out." One evening one of the men

Mary Elizabeth Badders. (*Courtesy May Overland.*)

showed up with a white starched linen suit on, and Mother started chasing after him and ran him through the kitchen . . . . He dove off out into the mud hole in the back where she threw the dishwater and where the pigs were. Boy, he was a mess!

As time went on, Mrs. Badders's persistence won out, for she was able to calm down her boarders, and she was also able to quiet down her rambunctious kids. At least May stopped throwing such lethal weapons. After all, she was growing up and needed to act more dignified. She even started helping her mother serve the food in the dining

Mary Elizabeth Norrid. (*Courtesy A. S. Norrid.*)

room, though not for long, because soon she fell in love and eloped with one of the boarders, a telegraph operator named William Overland:

> I was only 17, and I knew my parents wouldn't let me, so we ran off and got married. But we came right back, and I stayed in my room that night with my little niece. Nobody knew it until the next day when they read it in the paper. That's when everybody went wild! My husband

The City Hotel in the 1930s. *(Courtesy A. S. Norrid.)*

said, "Well, if you don't like it, I'll just take her and leave town." So Mother stopped yelling and actually cheered up because he started paying my board. Since I was now a paying guest, I didn't have to work anymore, but sometimes, in a pinch, I did help 'em anyway.

The Badders left the hotel around 1917 and moved to a large private residence they had bought from Kirby. But soon after moving there, Mrs. Badders was back in the boarding house business. "Kirby asked Mother to take some of the Harvey House* girls because it got too crowded in their quarters over the depot," said May. "And my husband and I went there for a while, too."

---

*The Harvey Houses were a chain of eating establishments and convenience stops stationed along the Santa Fe Railroad line in the late nineteenth and early twentieth centuries. See page 47.

The City Hotel in the early 1950s. (*Courtesy Eugenia Nixson.*)

There were distinct similarities between Mrs. Badders and her suc-
cessor, Mrs. Norrid. They both were named Mary Elizabeth, they both
raised young children while managing the hotel, and they both had
previous experience in operating boarding houses. Before moving to
Silsbee, Mrs. Norrid ran the City Hotel in Winnfield, Louisiana.
While in Winnfield, she and her husband Albert Sidney Norrid, who
was named after Civil War General Albert Sidney Johnston, adopted
their son A. S. after seeing his picture on the front page of the
Shreveport Times. "As soon as they saw that baby adoption advertise-
ment," A. S. laughed, "they knew they had to have me."

The Norrids were close friends of the Long family in Winnfield and
were often entertained by one of the Long boys, a very outgoing and
friendly young man who loved to visit the guests in the lobby of their
hotel there. Years later, after the Norrids moved to the hotel in Silsbee,
A. S. remembered that he and a friend went to Galveston for the
weekend, and while strolling along the seawall, they were surprised
to see a big black limousine pull over and stop. They were even more

The City Hotel after its final renovation. (*Courtesy Eugenia Nixson.*)

surprised when Huey P. Long, the boy from the days in Winnfield and now the famous U. S. Senator from Louisiana, got out and invited them to dinner at the Galvez Hotel. At the time, both boys were delighted by the invitation, but they were especially glad later that they had gotten to go because shortly thereafter, Long was assassinated.

One of Mary Norrid's first official acts at the Badders Hotel was to change its name to the City Hotel. Also, after the Norrids bought the hotel, they realized that the demand for rooms was greater than the supply, and added another building, which doubled the size.

Mrs. Norrid, a jovial woman who weighed 200 pounds, was a sharp contrast to her small, bald-headed, and rather serious husband. Despite their differences in temperament, they remained formally polite to each other at all times. "I never heard Dad call Mamma anything but 'wife' and Mamma always called Dad 'Mr. Norrid,'" A. S. reported. Maybe they just didn't have the time to get to know each other well enough to be on a first-name basis, because while Mrs. Norrid's time was consumed managing the large hotel, Mr. Norrid was busy with several other ventures. He worked in an auto mechanic shop, established the first bus route from Silsbee to Beaumont, operated a touring car business, served as justice of the peace for approximately twelve years, and later ran a mail route to several outlying communities.

Of all the boarders who stayed at the hotel during the Norrid's tenure, the carnival people, who came for the annual Hardin County Fair, were the most interesting. As a small boy, A. S. had been delighted by their adventures and thrilled by the "collateral" that they often left behind: "Nine times out of ten when they got ready to leave, they didn't have the money so Mamma would either hold their clothes or a diamond ring or whatever she could get."

A. S. was especially happy when his mother bargained for some of the trained animals in the shows. There was no denying that a monkey called Pete, a trick pony, and a parrot named Polly added interest to the daily lives of the young boy and boarders alike.

> One particular time, this gentleman had a monkey show. So, instead of holding his clothes or anything, Mamma took the monkey for me. Pete was quite a pet . . . . He and I got to be real good friends, and he would take up for me. My friends could make like they were going to hit me, and he would hit the end of the chain . . . one day, he was sitting on the back of a chair in the hotel, and Mamma came through the door carrying a glass of water in her hand. She didn't know the monkey was there, and the monkey reached over and caught her by the arm. When he did, it scared her, and she threw the glass of water in the monkey's face. After that, he hated her! We had to get rid of the monkey, or he would have torn her up.

> I don't remember the pony's name, but he would do tricks, all kinds of tricks . . . I could be riding him in town somewhere, and he'd decide to go home . . . . And I kept him until he got so mean that I had to get rid of him.

> Another time, she took this parrot in . . . and Polly had the run of the outdoors. Polly'd get up in this sycamore tree in the yard and call,

"Miz Norrid, Miz Norrid," and Mamma would go to the back porch and call back, "What do you want, Polly?" Then Polly'd say, "Come up here!"

Polly sounded just like Mamma . . . . This gentleman that she bought wood from drove up to the fence from time to time and would holler out, "Wood! Wood!" And, if Mamma needed some for her wood stove, she'd yell back, "Throw it over the fence." Well, one day Mamma was in town shopping or something, and the man drove his horse and wagon to the fence and hollered, "Wood!" And Polly hollered back, "Throw it over the fence!" So, he unloaded it and came after his money . . . no Mamma was there. He had to wait until Mamma came home to get his money, and I had to stack the wood.

The City Hotel gradually lost its prominence as the number one place in town to eat and sleep. Just as other hotels and boarding houses of the area had suffered at the hands of more rapid transportation, so did this long-standing establishment. The convenience of motels and fast food chains now fulfill the needs of the hurried traveler. Several years ago, the last of the boarders moved out and so did Mrs. Nixson. "I'd hoped to remain there the rest of my life," she told me. "But the repairs got to be too much."

Although John Henry Kirby's buildings may eventually all be gone, his legacy as a timber baron remains. And I'm sure that if he were alive today, he would be amused by Silsbee's notoriety as the car trading capital of Southeast Texas.

THE BADDERS HOTEL RECIPES

 MRS. BADDERS STEAMED FRUITCAKE
(John Henry Kirby's Favorite!)

After trying this recipe, I was convinced that John Henry Kirby knew more than just the timber business. He had to be pretty aware of the food business as well. At least, he knew who made the best fruit-cakes in town and never failed to place his order for several. May Overland told me that her mother, Mary Elizabeth Badders, used this recipe every Christmas—and it was considered old even then.

Since I knew it was going to be both time-consuming and expensive to make (approximately fifty dollars), I asked my mother, a fruitcake pro, and my friend Lynda Comeaux to help. Even with their assistance, it took two days to complete the baking.

Of course, Mrs. Badders used a wood stove for her cooking, but if you do not happen to have one, your modern range will do fine.

1¼ lbs. sugar
1¼ lbs. butter
1 tablespoon cinnamon
1 tablespoon nutmeg
yolks of 15 eggs, well-beaten
½ teacup molasses (slightly less than ½ measuring cup)
¼ teacup sherry
½ teacup whiskey or brandy
2¼ oz. strong lemon extract
1½ lbs. flour, sifted
3 lbs. raisins
2 lbs. currants (wash, soak overnight, and dry)
1 lb. candied cherries
1 lb. candied pineapple

1 lb. dates
1 lb. figs
1 lb. citron
¼ lb. lemon peel
¼ lb. orange peel
2 lbs. shelled pecan halves
whites of 15 eggs, stiffly beaten

Cream the sugar and butter. Add spices, yolks of the eggs, molasses, sherry, whiskey or brandy, and lemon extract. Set aside. Cut the fruits into large pieces (except raisins) and put in a large pan or bucket. Add pecan halves. Work in the fruits and nuts alternately with the flour. Stir in mixture which was set aside. Fold in stiffly beaten egg whites. Lightly grease twenty small (1 pound) rectangular pans , and line each pan with two layers of waxed paper on bottom and one layer on sides. Put batter in pans, filling ¾ of each pan. Cover each with foil and tie foil securely with string around top edge of pan. Place cakes on wire rack in a larger pan with a small amount of water in the bottom. Make sure that the pans are above the water. Cover the larger pan and steam for 4 to 4½ hours at 250°.

GINGER COOKIES

According to May Overland, ginger cookies were a must around the Badders Hotel because of her father's love for them.

    1 cup sugar
    1 cup brown sugar
    1 cup butter
    1 cup sorghum or ½ cup molasses and ½ cup pure
      cane syrup
    2 eggs, well-beaten
    1 tablespoon vinegar
    1 tablespoon vanilla
    1 tablespoon ginger
    3 teaspoons soda
    3 teaspoons salt
    5 cups flour

Cream sugars and butter. Add remaining ingredients. Shape dough into medium sized balls. Place on greased cookie sheet. Bake at 375° for 10 to 12 minutes.

THE CITY HOTEL RECIPES

Unfortunately, A. S. Norrid didn't have any of his mother's recipes to give me, but the next owner, Eugenia Nixson, had some excellent ones from her file.

 MRS. NIXSON'S CHILI BEANS

How about some delicious chili beans with thick brown gravy? "The secret," said Mrs. Nixson, "is to stir the beans a lot while they are cooking." They make a main dish when served with link sausage.

    2 lbs. pinto beans
    5 garlic sections, minced
    2 oz. chili powder
    1 tablespoon salt
    1½ teaspoons sugar
    smoked bacon or bacon drippings to season

Soak beans in water overnight and then drain off excess water. Place beans in large pot, cover with water, and add remaining ingredients. Cook until done. Stir often and add additional water if needed.

 YEAST ROLLS

On Sundays everybody from the churches came and ate, and there were a lot of schoolteachers that ate. We made yeast rolls all the time. Never plain biscuits or anything like that.

— *Eugenia Nixson*

2 cups buttermilk
1½ teaspoon salt
¼ cup sugar
3 teaspoons baking powder
⅔ cup vegetable oil
1 package dry yeast
1 cup lukewarm water
7 cups flour
flour to knead

Mix first 5 ingredients in a large bowl. Dissolve yeast in water and add to mixture. Add flour and knead. Sprinkle more flour over mixture as you knead to keep it from sticking to your hands. Grease a large bowl. Place dough in it, then lightly grease top of mixture to keep it from drying on top. Cover. Put in refrigerator. Take out any amount of dough as you need it. Knead down, roll out, and cut with a biscuit cutter. Grease tops of rolls with vegetable oil. Set out 30 minutes. Brush with melted butter. Bake in 400° oven until brown.

FRENCH-FRIED ONIONS

I've had guests tell me my onion rings were the best they had ever eaten. Some had eaten them in many places, even Mexico, but these were the best.

— *Eugenia Nixson*

1 cup sifted flour
1½ teaspoons baking powder
½ teaspoon salt
1 egg, slightly beaten
⅔ cup water
½ teaspoon lemon juice
1 tablespoon melted shortening
3 large onions cut into ¼ inch rings

Mix first 7 ingredients for batter. Dip a few onion rings at a time and fry for 2 minutes in hot oil.

 BUTTER CAKE

2 cups butter
2 cups sugar
3 cups sifted flour
2¼ teaspoons baking powder
pinch of salt
1 cup milk
1 teaspoon vanilla
8 egg whites, stiffly beaten

Cream butter and sugar well. Set aside. Sift flour with baking powder and salt. Add to butter mixture alternately with milk. Add vanilla. Fold in stiffly beaten egg whites. Grease and flour 10-inch tube pan and bake at 325° for approximately 1 hour and 15 minutes or until done.

Harvey House Restaurant in the Gulf, Colorado, and Santa Fe Train Terminal—Galveston, Texas, 1932. (*Courtesy Mr. Otis Thomas.*)

THE HARVEY HOUSES

H uman beings who have the urge to travel around from place to place are at the mercy of the elements. Even with the advent of the passenger train, which helped them escape some of the ravages of Mother Nature when traveling, they still had the inconveniences of erratic time schedules and substandard accommodations. Particularly in isolated areas like the Big Thicket, people were annoyed even more by half worn-out equipment and understaffed maintenance crews.

I can still remember the frustrations I felt the night I sat stalled on a train in the middle of nowhere. About a hundred other passengers and I waited for hours for the workmen to remove a cow who had moseyed over to the tracks to dine, and, while there, had dropped dead. As the clock ticked away, we were subjected to the stagnant heat and also to the droves of mosquitoes who feasted on us as well as on the carcass of the cow.

The Big Thicket was always the railroad's stepchild. The trains in the area rarely got any new equipment or supplies. Lon Wright, former agent for the Atchison, Topeka, and Santa Fe Railroad, confided, "About all that we ever got new were pencils and paper clips, and we didn't get very many of those either. We were always having to scrounge around for the most ordinary supplies; the only thing there was plenty of was complaints."

Harvey House Lunchroom— Silsbee, Texas, 1922. (*Courtesy Mr. Otis Thomas.*)

No matter how unpredictable the schedules or how uncomfortable the ride might have been on the Santa Fe, one thing that was always good was the dining car. As part of the Fred Harvey Company, the dining cars were operated under a contract agreement with the Santa Fe and were often able to afford the traveler with a bright spot in an otherwise dismal journey.

Traveling from Houston to Dallas, the highlight of the trip was eating lunch in the diner. It was expensive fare, but the pleasure from feeling sophisticated in posh surroundings made it worth every penny. Attentive waiters attired in crisp white dinner jackets served delicious food on lovely china plates. In addition, the spotless tablecloths and napkins, the silver flatware, and the serving pieces, along with the crystal glasses, inspired the traveler to display his best table manners.

Once while while traveling from Houston to Dallas, a waiter ushered a young boy to my table. As he was seated across from me, I noticed that he was holding a brown paper sack. When the attendant came for his order, he said, "I'll have a Coke." When the waiter placed the

Harvey House with hotel accommodations over the Santa Fe Depot—
Somerville, Texas, 1930s. (*Courtesy Mr. Otis Thomas.*)

Coke on the table, the boy reached into his sack and plopped a big
hamburger onto his plate. It was hard to tell which was the funniest
— the boy's pleased expression, the waiter's disgruntled one, or my
obviously amused one. There I had been soaking up the atmosphere
of these glamorous surroundings when, all of a sudden, I was jolted
out of my reverie back into reality. Oblivious to the reactions of the
onlookers, the boy just happily smacked away. I happened to catch
the waiter's eye and knew by his disapproving look that the boy had
intruded into his world, too, not necessarily into his world of fantasy,
but definitely into his world of economics. Something told me that
he knew that he wasn't going to get a tip out of this one!

From the late 1800s to the early 1900s, in addition to operating the
diners, the Fred Harvey Company also ran the Harvey Houses, which
were located approximately every 100 miles along the railroad line.
These included lunchrooms and restaurants, news and concession

stands, hotel rooms, and other accommodations. Everything portable belonged to the company, including dishes, cooking utensils, linens, and furniture. No matter what size an individual Harvey House was, each had the reputation for consistently providing unusually good food and good service. And if those were not enough to lift the spirits of even the weariest traveler, the neat and attractive young Harvey House waitresses were. Although some people considered them to be bold and risqué, the girls were generally well-bred, well-educated, and personable — the forerunners of today's airline stewardesses. Working for Fred Harvey gave these adventuresome young ladies the opportunity to see the country at the railroad's expense because they were issued free passes and given free meal tickets when traveling.

I was surprised to learn that there had once been a very large and elaborate Harvey House in Silsbee. Of course, during the early 1900s, Silsbee was a busy railroad terminal on the Santa Fe Line. The business was completely equipped with a lunchroom, a restaurant, and a basement with a barbershop and a poolroom. After it burned in 1920, it was replaced by a smaller lunchroom, which provided service until it closed in 1926.

Although I was unable to locate any former Harvey House girls in the area, I did interview Mr. Otis Thomas of Somerville, Texas, a former Harvey House employee. Mr. Thomas started out in the early '20s, in Silsbee as a cashier but became manager of one of the largest and nicest houses at the branch terminal of the Gulf, Colorado, and Santa Fe Railroad in Galveston. Mr. Thomas credited Fred Harvey with improving traveling accommodations along the Santa Fe. Railroad travel was at its height in America in 1850 when Harvey immigrated to America from England at the age of fifteen. But the boy was shocked over the obviously inferior food and service available then. He went from washing dishes to owning a restaurant in just a few years, and by 1876, he opened the first Harvey House in Topeka, Kansas. His food service company flourished until 1929. The Depression years, coupled with the development of faster travel, finally brought about his company's decline. Today it is a division of Amfac, a Hawaiian-based corporation. After talking with several Santa Fe officials, it is my

Dee Husband, fry cook, and Otis Thomas, cashier—Silsbee, Texas, 1922.
(*Courtesy Mr. Otis Thomas.*)

understanding that the Fred Harvey name is still being used at various resort areas: a resort in Death Valley, a recreational hotel at the Petrified Forest Painted Desert, and the El Tovar Hotel at the Grand Canyon. Some of the original buildings are still standing, but they are either vacant or used for other purposes.

I am sorry that the passenger trains across the country have virtually faded away. Even when considering the frustrating hours I spent on that train the night the cow died on the tracks, it was still preferable to the horrors of city traffic.

HARVEY HOUSES RECIPES

In recent years, the city of Galveston has become more than a seaside resort of sandy beaches, dining establishments, and shell shops. Thanks to the work of the Galveston Historical Society, visitors can now tour restored homes and mansions, some of which date back to before the infamous storm of 1900 which destroyed much of the island, and can browse through the unique stores along the Strand, the city's oldest business district. At the north end of the Strand is the Railroad Museum that was once the branch headquarters of the Gulf, Colorado, and Santa Fe Railroad and the home of one of the seventy-two original Harvey House restaurants. Although the restaurant wasn't included in the museum's restoration project, an old blueprint of the terminal still exists, and I hope one day tourists can experience the nostalgia of early twentieth-century dining at its best.

According to Mr. Otis Thomas, who was manager of the Galveston Harvey House from 1929 to 1936, the food throughout the system was consistently good because the officials at the main office in Kansas City, Missouri, controlled its operation by a centralized form of strict management. It was there that all final decisions were made, all the choice meats were selected and shipped in ice, and all the managers and chefs were trained. Managers were issued a manual of recipes and instructions that explained every detail of food preparation from the heating of the serving plates to the garnishing of special dishes. By frequently visiting each establishment along the line, Fred Harvey officials kept watch over the whole operation.

I couldn't believe my good fortune when I discovered that Mr. Thomas had saved his instruction book from Galveston and graciously agreed to allow me to use it. After checking several other sources, I decided this may be the only book of original Harvey House recipes around today, and therefore, a real treasure. I have tried many of the recipes, and so far I haven't found a bad one in the lot.

A ZESTY APPETIZER

1 – 3¼ oz. can sardines (sardines in hot chilies are good)
2 tablespoons anchovy paste
1 teaspoon grated onion
Worcestershire sauce
mayonnaise
white sandwich bread, trimmed
cream cheese

Remove bones from sardines. Mash with a fork, then mix with anchovy paste. Add onions, dash of Worcestershire sauce, and enough mayonnaise for spreading. Lay several trimmed bread slices on dampened cup towel. Spread with sardine mixture and roll like a jelly roll. Slice into sections, place on cookie sheet, and toast. Top with softened cream cheese.

 TOMATO-CHEESE SALAD

1 small box lime gelatin*
1 tablespoon unflavored gelatin
2 cups boiling water
2 small packages cream cheese
1 can tomato soup, undiluted
1 tablespoon chopped onion
1 cup chopped green pepper
1 cup finely chopped celery
cayenne pepper to taste

Dissolve gelatins in boiling water. Cool slightly. Add cream cheese and tomato soup and beat until mixture is blended. Cool completely, then fold in chopped vegetables. Season with cayenne pepper. Pour into mold and cool until firm. Unmold, serve on crisp lettuce leaves, and top with mayonnaise.

---

*I substituted lemon gelatin for the lime gelatin listed in the original recipe because I liked the color better when it was mixed with the tomato soup.

 CLAM CHOWDER

4 – 10 oz. cans whole clams
½ lb. salt pork, diced
2 medium onions, chopped
1 cup celery, chopped
1 green pepper, chopped
4 medium potatoes, diced
½ teaspoon thyme
1 bay leaf, crumbled
salt and pepper to taste
3 tablespoons flour, stirred into ⅓ cup water
2 cups milk
2 cups cream
2 tablespoons butter
paprika

Drain clams and set aside both clams and broth. Fry diced pork until crisp. Remove meat and set it aside. Sauté onions in pork fat until lightly browned. Transfer onions and pork fat to a four-quart pot. Add clams, celery, green pepper, potatoes, thyme, bay leaf, and salt and pepper. Pour in broth saved from clams plus enough boiling water to make 3 cups of liquid. Stir in flour mixture. Cover pot and simmer for 30 minutes. Add milk, cream, and butter. Heat, but do not boil. Add more salt and pepper if desired. Sprinkle crumbled pork and paprika on top and serve.

For a different taste, add 1 can (14½ oz.) of whole tomatoes and substitute 4 cups of water for the milk and cream.

Serve with a tart green salad and cheese biscuits for a special light lunch.

CREAMED STUFFED EGGS

6 eggs, hard-boiled
salt, pepper, chopped chives, and mayonnaise to taste
white sauce
3 tablespoons chopped pimento
3 tablespoons deviled ham
parsley

Cut cold hard-boiled eggs in half, lengthwise. Mash yolks, and add salt, pepper, chopped chives, and mayonnaise to taste. Stuff whites. Put halves together to look whole or serve in halves as preferred. Make a rich medium thick white sauce. Add pimento and deviled ham to sauce and stir. Pour sauce over eggs and reheat. Serve hot and garnish with parsley.

WHITE SAUCE

Melt 4 tablespoons butter in saucepan. Blend in 3 to 4 tablespoons flour. Add 2 cups of milk and ½ teaspoon salt and a dash of pepper and continue cooking until thick, stirring constantly.

CHEESE BISCUITS

½ cup butter
1 ½ cups flour
1 lb. sharp cheddar cheese, grated
salt and cayenne pepper to taste

Mix all ingredients, roll into small-sized balls, and bake on greased cookie sheet at 400° for ten to fifteen minutes.

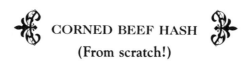

CORNED BEEF HASH
(From scratch!)

You don't even have to wait until St. Patrick's Day to enjoy this dish.

    3 lbs. corned beef brisket
    freshly crushed black pepper
    4 potatoes, chopped
    1 green pepper, chopped
    5 stalks of celery, chopped
    1 large onion, chopped
    salt and cayenne pepper to taste

Season corned beef brisket generously with crushed black pepper and place in a pot. Cover with water, bring to a boil, and lower temperature to medium heat. Cover pot and gently boil brisket for approximately 3½ hours or until tender. Remove meat from broth and set broth aside. Coarsely grind meat in a food chopper. Put chopped meat in skillet. Chop all the vegetables and add to meat, along with salt and cayenne pepper to taste. Add enough stock to mixture to moisten well. Cover skillet and simmer approximately 30 minutes. Divide and put into 4 individual baking dishes and brown in oven.

CORNED BEEF HASH AND EGGS

Many recipes in the chef's cooking manual contained additional instructions and comments from the central office such as the following:

This is a nice dish, not only for breakfast but very appropriate for the noonday bill. In fact, not objectionable for service throughout the twenty-four hours of the day.

We have had this on trial at two or three of the houses with very favorable reports, and if you see that it is made according to above, it should be very good. Do not permit any guessing. As a matter of fact, our cooks do too much guessing as to quantities, and, in my opinion, there is no reason why our cooks should not be as careful in compounding foods as a druggist is in compounding his medicine. I say this with all respect for the discriminating taste which we all recognize as being also most important, but I am giving you the exact amounts for the benefit of those who are lacking in tastes.

For a good breakfast dish, put corned beef hash into individual serving dishes and hollow out the center. Place 2 raw eggs in the hollowed area and bake at 375° until eggs are cooked to desired firmness.

 CHEESE SOUFFLÉ

6 tablespoons butter
9 tablespoons flour
3 cups grated sharp cheddar cheese
dash cayenne pepper
9 eggs, separated

Melt butter in top part of double boiler. Add flour, cheese, and cayenne pepper. Mix and remove from heat. Add well-beaten egg yolks. Cool mixture slightly, then fold in stiffly beaten egg whites. Turn into a buttered baking dish, place dish in a pan of hot water, and bake for 20 to 25 minutes in a 350° oven. (This is better if it doesn't become too firm.)

BEEF RISSOLES WITH MASHED POTATOES

3 lbs. lean beef roast seasoned with salt and pepper
1 green pepper, chopped
1 small onion, chopped
3 cups boiled rice
1 teaspoon savory seasoning
½ teaspoon nutmeg
1 teaspoon grated lemon peel
salt and pepper to taste
bread crumbs

Boil seasoned beef until tender. Reserve stock. Grind meat and add chopped vegetables, rice, and seasonings. Form in balls about the size of small hen eggs. Add a little more beef stock if needed for moisture. Bread meatballs and fry. Serve 4 balls on each mound of mashed potatoes topped with good brown gravy.

MASHED POTATOES

Peel and chop 5 potatoes and place in pot of salted water. Boil until tender, drain liquid, and mash. Add butter and small amount of canned milk and whip. Stir in desired amount of salt and pepper.

 BROWN GRAVY

Pour a small amount of beef stock into a skillet and heat. Stir in enough flour to make paste. Brown until dark. Add warm water and cook until mixture makes gravy. Season with salt and pepper.

Additional comments from the Harvey House main office were:

Please do not forget that it is not only a matter of cooking these dishes right, but it is also a question of making the sales. This can be done only by your girls actually calling the attention of the patron to this particular dish. You can stimulate the interest of your girls by inquiring after each meal just how many dishes they sold. If such dishes are well made after the patron once buys, he will purchase the second time without his attention having been directed to it.

 MAYONNAISE

Harvey House restaurants were known for making their own delicious salad dressings. After trying several of the ones listed in the chef's manual, I selected this tart mayonnaise recipe. It's easy to prepare and its distinct flavor makes it different from anything you can buy.

2 eggs
1 tablespoon dry mustard
¾ teaspoon salt
½ teaspoon white pepper
¼ teaspoon red pepper
1 tablespoon flour
2 cups salad oil
3 tablespoons boiling water
2 tablespoons fresh lemon juice

Put eggs into mixing bowl. Add the next 5 ingredients. Mix until thoroughly blended. Slowly add salad oil. When mayonnaise thickens, add boiling water and lemon juice. Mix thoroughly.

PECAN TORTE

4 eggs, well-beaten
1 lb. brown sugar
1 cup flour
1½ teaspoons baking powder
1 cup pecans, chopped
1 teaspoon vanilla

Mix all ingredients, pour into two 9-inch well-greased and floured cake pans, and bake at 325° for 30 to 35 minutes. Cool completely before removing from pans. The layers will be thin.

Filling:

1 tablespoon butter
2 teaspoons flour
1 cup whipped cream
5 teaspoons sugar
1 cup pecans, chopped

Melt butter in top of double boiler. Blend in flour, stir in whipped cream, and cook until thick. Cool. Add sugar and nuts. Spread mixture between layers of torte.

Icing:

2 cups sweetened whipped cream
½ cup pecans, chopped

Ice top and sides of torte with whipped cream and sprinkle top with chopped nuts.

John Henry Kirby.

B E S S M A Y

THE BESSMAY HOTEL

L umberman John Henry Kirby
created Bessmay, another saw-
mill town, on the eastern edge of the Thicket. The sawmill there was
the largest of the early Kirby mills and seemed to have John Henry
Kirby's personal stamp all over it, even to being named for his only
child. According to Mr. Homer Holland, Bessmay's last mill foreman,
the mill produced around 160,000 board feet of lumber a day and was
the first mill to start up again after the Depression. Also, it was in
the Bessmay Hotel that a toddler who was to become a celebrity long
after she left Bessmay, first attracted attention.

I visited the town in the fall of 1984, when former resident Mrs.
Mable Bray invited me to one of the semi-annual Bessmay Cemetery
Homecoming reunions. There, I was able to find out for myself the
details of the town's exciting past. Looking around, I realized that the
forest had rightfully reclaimed much of the territory usurped in 1901
by Kirby's workmen. Like so many of the early forest towns, it now
exists only in the memories of those who lived there. Fortunately,
those were the people I met at the homecoming. Their love for the
area and their concern for their family members' graves and the attention they gave to the upkeep of the graves enhanced the natural beauty
of the cemetery. Although I had been to many other homecomings,
I will never forget that one because it was the first time that I had

observed survivors of that by-gone era take time to pay their respects, cleaning the graves and reminiscing about the past. From them, I learned about Bessmay.

Naturally, I was mainly interested in gathering information about the hotel, but I was amused by Ed Reichelt and Bill Skinner and their accounts of a Halloween prank they and some of their mischievous friends played a long time ago. According to them, early in the century, groceries were delivered from the Kirby Commissary in a wagon drawn by two mules. One Halloween they painted the mules to resemble zebras and dismantled the wagon and rebuilt it atop the commissary. According to Reichelt and Skinner, it didn't take anyone long to figure out who did it, and the culprits were rapidly put to work undoing their wrongdoings. The boys had the last laugh, though, because it took a long time for the paint to wear off those mules. In the meantime, the animals were so disoriented that when they were put out to pasture, neither one of them could recognize the other, and they wandered around in a daze, helplessly looking for a familiar face.

The hotel, built in 1901, was closed temporarily during the Depression but otherwise remained operational until 1950. Since the Bessmay mill was the biggest of Kirby's nine mills, this hotel needed to be large enough to accommodate a host of single mill workers and school-teachers, as well as John Henry himself. On his trips to the mill, he stayed in special rooms reserved for his exclusive use in the back of the hotel, and enjoyed the wonderful down-home cooking served by Lizzie Collins, long-time manager of the hotel.

Kirby and his group of Northern investors owned the Kirby mill towns completely—from the actual mills and commissaries to the private residences. Everything but the mill worker's soul seemed to have "JHK" stamped visibly across it, and even that exception was debatable. Kirby employees were usually paid in paper scrip rather than cash, which could be redeemed at full market value only at the Kirby Commissary, making it possible for some of the workers to "owe their soul[s] to the company store," to paraphrase Tennessee Ernie Ford's hit song. This feudal system, a holdover from the medieval times, was a guarantee that no one except John Henry Kirby and his partners would get rich.

Mrs. Nancy Price in front of the Bessmay Hotel, 1921.
(Courtesy Mrs. Viola Musgrove St. Ores.)

At least, the abundance of sawmill towns in the area afforded the worker the luxury of being able to politely suggest that his employer "take this job and shove it!" (another hit song). There were generally always jobs available a few miles down the road if one chose to leave. Most of the time, though, John Henry was able to keep his employees happy by exhibiting small but important gestures of good will.

Kirby's sidekick in Bessmay was a notorious character named Joe Marriott. Ed Reichelt remembered him well and described him as being an ultraconservative. "He thought we were going to hell with all this 'liberal stuff.' Marriott never married, never took a drink, never smoked a cigarette, never had sex, and he associated mainly with a pack of dogs that followed him around. He didn't even know what the touch of a woman was! That to me is unbelievable!"

Between the two of them, Kirby and Marriott kept a finger on the pulse of the community, and in keeping with a policy borrowed from King Henry IV of France of "a chicken in his pot every Sunday," Kirby's benevolence took the form of a turkey on every table at Christmas along with a Bible and gift for every child. Kirby's benevolence was also extended to more than one young man who were given funds to attend college.

Bessmay may not be on the map today, but in its prime, all kinds of unexpected things happened there. In 1913 a former resident of the Bessmay Hotel was kidnapped—an event which was still making newspaper headlines in the 1930s and again as recently as 1982. In fact, the kidnapping was more noteworthy several years later than it was when it actually happened.

In 1913, it was very unusual for a car to be seen in Bessmay, so it would have been strange for anyone in the neighborhood not to have observed a long black automobile rolling slowly past the rows of company houses. The car slowed to a stop in front of the house where a beautiful golden-haired toddler played quietly by herself. Getting out of the car, an attractive woman ran up to the porch where the child sat preoccupied in her world of make-believe and said, "Come on, Virginia, let's go for a ride." The little girl, interrupted in her play, looked at the woman. Puzzled at first, her expression of surprise rapidly turned into a smile as she ran to the woman with outstretched arms calling, "Mackie, Mackie!" Although the little girl was grimy and disheveled, the woman excitedly embraced her before carrying her back to the car. Until the week before, the child, Virginia Katherine McMath, and her father had been residents of the Bessmay Hotel. Her mother, Lela McMath, had separated from her husband and was pursuing a career in North Texas, so Virginia had remained behind with her father and her nurse, May Phillips. Because Miss Phillips loved the child and took exceptionally good care of her, Lela McMath agreed to the arrangement, provided the child did not live with her paternal grandmother.

The time Virginia had lived in the hotel was well spent, and actually served as a first training ground for her future. While she and her father resided there, the other boarders had come to love the little child who entertained them tirelessly. Her father often took her to the old lodge hall for Saturday night get-togethers, where she picked up the dance steps better and quicker than any of the adults. Every night, the boarders could look forward to Virginia's renditions of the latest dances. They were delighted by the child's antics and were sorry to see her move to a private house to be cared for by her grandmother. When the mother discovered that Virginia was living with her grandmother, she went to Bessmay and "kidnapped" her daughter. Soon afterwards, Lela McMath married a Mr. Rogers. Years later, people in Bessmay were thrilled to learn that Virginia McMath, the golden-haired girl who had tapped her way into their hearts, then been taken away, had grown into the famous dancer, Ginger Rogers, and was now dancing in the hearts of all America.

BESSMAY HOTEL RECIPES

Good food may not have played a major role in Homer and Irene Holland's courtship, but their romance started around one of the dining tables in the Bessmay Hotel while they boarded there. Mr. Holland said "the food was the best in the world." Now, after a marriage of more than fifty years, Mr. and Mrs. Holland still remember the early years at the Bessmay.

 STEW

A lot of people used leftovers to make stew, but Mrs. Collins never served us leftovers. Her stew always was made from fresh foods.
— *Irene Holland*

    2 lbs. beef stew meat
    salt and pepper
    6 cups water
    1 tablespoon bacon drippings
    1 onion, chopped
    4 tomatoes, chopped
    3 white potatoes, chopped
    3 ears of corn, shucked
    ½ cup rice

Season meat generously with salt and pepper and place in large pot along with water and bacon drippings. Boil meat gently until tender (approximately 3 hours). Add onion, tomatoes, potatoes, and corn. Cook 30 minutes. Add rice and continue cooking an additional 20 minutes.

FRESH SHELLED PEAS

My roommate wouldn't eat peas on Sundays at all—cabbage or turnip greens or anything like that. He said, "I'll eat that six days a week, so I'm not going to eat it on Sunday." He would eat chicken and dumplings and fried chicken and stuff like that. Sunday meals he called them. Pervis Walton was his name. We called him "Spot."
— *Homer Holland*

4 cups shelled peas
water
salt to taste
bacon drippings, sliced bacon, or salt pork

Wash peas, place them in a pot, and cover them with water. Add salt and meat seasoning. Bring peas to a boil, reduce heat, cover pot, and boil gently until peas are tender.

 VANILLA CUSTARD ICE CREAM

7 eggs, well beaten
2 cups sugar
pinch of salt
4 cups milk
1 can sweetened condensed milk
1 large can evaporated milk
2 teaspoons vanilla

Put eggs, sugar, salt, and milk in large pot and cook over low heat until scalded well, stirring frequently. Add the 2 cans of milk and vanilla. Mix well. Freeze in a freezer for approximately 45 minutes, using 5 cups of ice to each ¼ cup of ice cream salt. Pour off the salt water, remove the excess ice, and wipe top before removing any ice cream.

To harden ice cream, replace top with cork, cover with ice, sprinkle with ice cream salt, and let it set.

 JELLY CAKE

Pervis wasn't the only one who looked forward to Mrs. Collins's Sunday meals. Homer and Irene did, too. According to them, the old-fashioned jelly cakes, chocolate pies, and vanilla ice cream just couldn't be beat.

Jelly cake was baked in thin layers which were iced with an ample amount of jelly. Blackberry jelly was used most often, but other jellies such as mayhaw were sometimes substituted. The cake was always better after it would "set" a day for the layers to absorb the jelly.

    2 cups sugar
    1 cup butter
    4 eggs
    1 cup milk
    3 cups flour
    2 teaspoons baking powder
    pinch of salt
    jelly

Cream sugar and butter. Beat in eggs. Add milk, flour, baking powder, and salt. Stir. Grease and flour five cake pans. Pour equal amounts of batter into pans for thin layers. Bake at 375° for approximately 20 to 25 minutes. Cool, remove from pans, and spread jelly between layers and on top of cake.

CHOCOLATE PIE

1 cup sugar
2½ tablespoons flour
2½ tablespoons cocoa
3 egg yolks
1½ cups milk
3 tablespoon butter
1 teaspoon vanilla
1 pie shell, baked

Combine sugar, flour, cocoa. Beat egg yolks and milk, and add to first mixture. Cook in double boiler, stirring constantly until thick. Stir in vanilla and add butter and cool. Pour into baked pie shell. (See East Texas Hotel recipes for pie crust recipe.) Top with meringue. Bake at 375° until golden brown.

 MERINGUE

3 egg whites
⅛ teaspoon cream of tartar
6 tablespoons sugar

Beat egg whites (room temperature) with cream of tartar and baking powder until frothy. Gradually beat in the sugar. Continue beating until stiff and glossy.

Mattie Scott. *(Courtesy Alfreida Foster.)*

THE SCOTT HOTEL

While there were numerous hotels throughout the Big Thicket during the early part of the century for the convenience of white travelers, accomodations for blacks were almost nonexistent. Of course, the prevailing attitude of southern whites toward blacks hadn't progressed much since the years of slavery, so with the possible single exception of servants, blacks were excluded from the privilege of dining, much less residing, in any of the white establishments. Since I was perplexed about the available provisions for the blacks, I began to ask questions which were usually answered rather nonchalantly. "Oh, I guess they made out somehow . . . . They must've stayed in people's houses," were remarks that I heard. But what about the black traveler who had to spend the night in a strange town where he didn't know anyone? Surely, there were more than just haphazard accommodations in existence. My first clue that a hotel for blacks existed came while I was browsing in an antique store in Trinity, a small town on the northwestern edge of the Big Thicket. As I stood admiring a lovely old chandelier, I was told that the fixture had once hung in the dining room of the Scott Hotel, an establishment for blacks which had been in operation years earlier.

The more that I heard about Walter Scott and his wife Mattie, owners of the hotel, the more I wanted to know. Scott had been the only black man in Trinity to attend an all-white church, and he always

made his presence known. "He'd sit in the balcony, and when the collection plate was passed around, he'd thump a coin real hard on the edge of the plate so that the congregation below would know that he was there," somebody told me. I'm sure the preacher was thrilled to have Scott visit his church because after the others heard the thump, they probably all dug a little deeper into their pockets. Scott was always a great believer in preparing for the future, too, so much so that he even bought his own casket fifteen years before he needed it and kept it in his living room for everybody to admire. Of course, after hearing all that, I had to find somebody who could tell me about the Scotts.

It seemed to take forever to locate anyone who'd actually lived there, but finally, over a year later, I met Hortense Green and Alfreida Foster, nieces of the Scotts. They, along with at least nine of their cousins, grew up at the hotel and were happy to tell me about it.

Hortense and Alfreida are well-educated women who emphasized the importance of strong moral values and conduct. Both learned from the Scotts that a little determination and imagination go a long way toward producing tangible rewards. The son of a wealthy former slave-owner and an impoverished former slave, Walter Scott began his unusual career as a mail rider between Trinity and Moscow. By the 1890s he realized that Trinity would offer many financial opportunities associated with the railroad, so it was there that he decided to build his future.

With little money at the beginning, but a big desire to succeed, Scott started his first business venture there. He bought an old mule and wagon and went into the draying business, but it wasn't long before he had so much work that the mule wore out and the wagon fell apart. Fortunately, though, he had already earned enough to invest in other things. Pretty soon, he had a whole new collection of money-makers: he bought two new mules and two new wagons, a jitney for transporting people to other towns, a truck for making deliveries, and a fine hotel to accommodate all those blacks who had to stay in Trinity overnight before catching an early morning train.

Walter Scott. *(Courtesy Alfreida Foster.)*

Walter and Mattie Scott were proud of the advanced accommodations they offered their guests during a time when even low-quality services were generally in short supply to the black traveler. Excellent meals were always served on beautiful china with cut-glass crystal, embroidered napkins, and napkin rings. And then there was the ultimate in modern luxury, running water. Naturally, since this was long before any of the other black hotels or—come to think of it—most of the white hotels had indoor plumbing, his was a landmark achievement. According to Alfreida, her Aunt Mattie was a woman of fiery temperament.

Why, there couldn't be a speck of dust anywhere, and once she had me take salt pork back to the grocer and change it for bacon 'cause she said "only poor folks eat salt pork, and don't you never forget it!"

In addition to having a strict code for her own conduct, Mattie also expected and usually got the best from those around her.

We had a cook once that we called Miss Kitty. Sometimes right in the middle of the time we were gettin' dinner on the table, she'd decide the Spirit had hit her, and she'd start dancin'. Boy! She could pull that dress up to here and do the biggest buck 'n wing you'd ever seen in your life. She'd say, "Thank God, Almighty!! Thank God, the Spirit got me!"

You see, she was Sanctified. That's a religion among some of the black folks. She'd always wear white 'cause she said that meant she was pure and holy. Well, all her religious finaglin' and messin' up the dinner at the wrong time, or maybe I should say just at the right time to get out of work, soon got her into big trouble with my obviously unsanctified Aunt Mattie. One day, right in the middle of one of her dances, Mattie said, "Miss Kitty, you just take your spirit and just get outa here, and don't you never come back 'cause if you do, I'm gonna take this skillet here and santify you over the head and your dancin' days'll be over forever!"

Aunt Mattie didn't ever put up with much foolishness, particularly when it came to some of her guests trying to pull something over on her. If a man and woman came to sign the register that they were married and she found out that they weren't, she'd march right into their room even in the middle of 'whatever!' and make 'em leave right then! It wasn't a matter of suggestin' . . . it was a matter of demandin' that they get their bags and get out!!!

Mattie, fiery and outspoken, and Walter, calm and reserved, were very compatible in spite of their personality differences. The key to their congeniality lay in their mutual desire to make life better for the people they loved. Hortense credits their intervention in her life as

Alfreida Foster in front of the Scott Hotel. (*Courtesy Alfreida Foster.*)

having made all the difference in the world. She maintains that without them, none of the kids would have amounted to a "hill of beans." Although she says that she started life "dirt poor," she gratefully remembers Walter and Mattie for having satisfied her hungry appetite, not only for good food but also for a good education. In addition, they taught her the value of seeing the lighter side of life:

> On one particular day, one of Uncle Walter's mules decided he wasn't gonna pull, so Lemmie, the boy who worked for Uncle Walter, took a whip and started beatin' the mule, and the mule fell and died. So, someone went to Uncle Walter and told him, "Mr. Scott, Lemmie killed ya' mule!" Uncle Walter just looked at the man for a while and then asked, "He did?" "Yeah," said the man, "Ol' Bess is dead." Uncle Walter waited a minute and then finally said, "Well, Ol' Bess is dead. I guess I'm gonna have to buy me another one . . . buy me another mule . . . and buy me another nigger!"

For years, the daily routine continued, with Walter hauling and with Mattie cooking, cleaning, and sometimes helping deliver babies down at the Barnes clinic. Both continued to teach their adopted brood the value of honesty and the merit of hard work. And every evening, Walter would come home, relax in his easy chair, and, just as if he had never thought it or said it before, announce that "time and tide waits for no one!"

He must have believed in what he was saying because in 1921, years before his time ran out and his tide came in, Walter sold his draying business and retired so that he could enjoy the fruits of his labor. His labors had paid off both emotionally, evidenced by his happy family, and financially. "He had a good bit of valuable property and plenty of cash," said Alfreida, "enough to be listed in Dun and Bradstreet, or so I heard." With some of the proceeds, he and Mattie bought a car and hired a chauffeur, and the trio spent three months touring the United States.

The most important legacy they left was not material but involved a sense of values they instilled in all who knew them. Whether they were working, worshipping, or playing, the Scotts had an appreciation for life and a style of living that made them truly unforgettable.

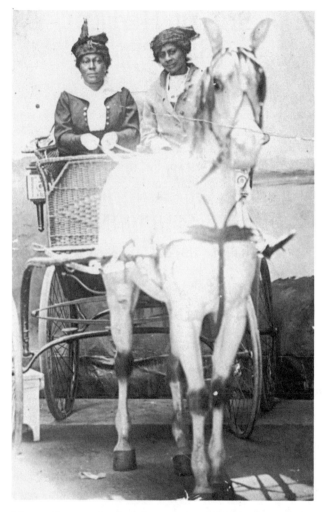

Mattie Scott and a friend going for a Sunday buggy ride.
(Courtesy Alfreida Foster.)

Scott Hotel
Recipes

In the days before refrigeration, beef was not eaten as often as it is today. When a cow was butchered, the meat had to be eaten quickly, so it was usually sold or traded among neighbors. Most rural folks like the Scotts had a milk cow or two, but it was a lot cheaper and faster to fatten chickens and hogs than cattle.

 PAN-FRIED STEAK

When beef was available, this dish was popular.

    2 lbs. thickly-sliced round steak
    salt and pepper
    flour
    1 cup buttermilk
    1 egg, beaten
    1 cup flour
    1 teaspoon baking powder
    bacon drippings

Cut meat into serving pieces and season with salt and pepper. Pound (to tenderize) at least ½ cup flour into meat with edge of heavy plate. Mix buttermilk and beaten egg together in one bowl. Mix 1 cup flour and baking powder together in another. Dip meat into egg mixture and then dredge in flour mixture. Heat bacon drippings in skillet until hot and brown meat on both sides. Serve with cream gravy.

CREAM GRAVY

Pour approximately 4 tablespoons of bacon drippings into a skillet and heat. Add 4 tablespoons of flour, stirring until slightly brown. Gradually add 2 cups of milk and stir until mixture thickens. Salt and pepper to taste.

OKRA AND TOMATOES

1 large onion, chopped
½ cup bacon drippings
3 large tomatoes, cut up
4 cups okra, sliced crosswise
1 tablespoon sugar
salt and pepper to taste

In a skillet brown onion in drippings. Add tomatoes and okra and cook slowly for about 10 minutes. Add sugar, salt, and pepper. Cover skillet and continue cooking until tender.

 **PEAR PRESERVES**

We had a farm on the outskirts of town, and we raised a garden. We didn't have to buy anything like eggs and vegetables. We had fruit trees and made our own preserves.

— *Hortense Green.*

3 quarts of pears
4½ cups of sugar
3 cups of water
lemon

Wash, peel, trim, and slice 3 quarts of pears. Combine 4 ½ cups of sugar with 3 cups of water and pour into a large pot. Boil rapidly for approximately 5 minutes until mixture makes a light syrup. Cool liquid slightly, add pears, and boil gently for 30 minutes. Add lemon slices from 1 lemon to retard darkening, and continue cooking until fruit is tender (about 2 ½ hours). Remove from heat, cover pot, and let the fruit stand overnight.

The next day take fruit out and pack in hot, sterilized pint jars. Heat syrup until boiling. Cover fruit with hot syrup and seal.

 VINEGAR PIE

Our noonday meals were always served at 12 o'clock sharp and there was never a meal without some kind of hot bread and a dessert. Sometimes when there wasn't anything else, Aunt Mattie would make vinegar pies. They were good, too.

— *Alfreida Foster*

    ½ cup butter
    2 cups sugar
    4 eggs, separated
    ¼ cup vinegar
    pie crust, lightly browned

Cream butter and sugar. Add well-beaten egg yolks and vinegar. Fold in stiffly beaten egg whites. Pour filling into 8-inch pie shell and bake approximately 45 minutes or until filling sets at 350°. (See page 118 for pie crust recipe.)

BAKING POWDER BISCUITS

2 cups flour
4 teaspoons baking powder
½ teaspoon baking soda
1 teaspoon salt
½ cup cold shortening
1 cup buttermilk

Sift dry ingredients and stir. Cut in shortening until it resembles coarse meal. Add buttermilk gradually and mix into soft dough. Place on floured board and knead gently. Roll dough lightly to a ½ inch thickness. Cut with a biscuit cutter and place on an ungreased cookie sheet. Bake at 450° until brown.

 LYE SOAP

It was always my job to make our lye soap because everyone else pretended that they didn't know how. It was done outside in our big old cast iron wash pot and would take you a good half a day to make. I had to make it quite often especially during hog killing time.

— *Hortense Green*

You don't have to own a wash pot to make lye soap. It can be made in your kitchen in a big pot. Start by saving fat drippings in glass quart jars. (I asked a manager of a big meat market to save me the fat and then I rendered it.) When 4 jars have been filled, remove the grease from the jars and put into a pot (not aluminum or glass.) Clean the grease by boiling it with an equal amount of water. Remove from heat and slowly stir in 1 quart of cold water. Remove fat when top gets firm. Dissolve one 13-ounce can of lye in 2½ pints cold water by slowly adding the lye to the water. (Protect your hands with rubber gloves and stand as far as possible from the pot to avoid breathing fumes.) Stir with a wooden spoon. Melt fat and let it cool gradually, stirring occasionally. Pour lye solution very slowly into the melted fat, stirring carefully. Continue stirring for approximately 15 minutes until it becomes the consistency of thick honey. Pour into a long pan. Set aside, let cool, cut into bars and let dry out.

Jesse Bill Barnes, Cecile Cariker and Mrs. Nora Cariker in
front of the Cariker Hotel, 1937. This hotel was torn down
in 1939 and replaced by a new one in the same year.
(Courtesy Mrs. W. B. Cariker.)

THE CARIKER HOTEL

W hen boarding houses through-out the Big Thicket began to be closed in the 1930s and '40s, Mrs. Nora Cariker, long-time owner of the Cariker Hotel in Kountze, used her innovative talents and determined spirit to keep her doors open. By emphasizing good food more than lodging accommodations, she started serving lunch to the town's working people, catering to special evening groups, and preparing Sunday feasts fit for a king. People came from miles around, and before anyone knew it, this small town entrepreneur had turned her dying business into one of the best eating places in the piney woods.

The hotel, which was down the road from the older Commercial Hotel and close to the courthouse, started off around 1906 as the Flora Hotel. It later became the Sims Hotel, but by the early 1920s, Mrs. Cariker and her husband, Mr. W. P. Cariker, owned it. Some of the most colorful reminiscences about the Cariker come from these early boarding house days.

My mother, Minnie Burwick, moved to the hotel as a nineteen-year-old schoolteacher after accepting her first teaching job in Kountze. Although she had gone away to college, this was, for all practical purposes, her first trip out into the world alone—or so she thought. Of course, she wasn't actually alone because Mrs. Cariker immediately began treating her more like a daughter than an ordinary guest.

My mother must have really felt special at the hotel because of all the care that she received. Her room was next to the Cariker family quarters, she ate at their table in the dining room, and she always had a special after-school snack waiting for her. It was a lucky thing that she got all this homey attention because she certainly had her hands full that first year. Some of Mother's students were older than she was, but back then, you could become a teacher after only two years of college. A few of the boys in the area figured that if they played around in school longer, they could play around in sports longer. Consequently, beginning teachers were sometimes younger than some of their students. Not only was she teaching some boys who were older than she, but she was also being pursued by one of the town's most eligible young bachelors—my father, Lester Crews.

One of Mother's fondest memories revolved around John Foster, the crippled black hired man who lived behind the hotel in a shack and caused Mrs. Cariker all kinds of aggravation while doing odd jobs for her. According to Versie Johnson, another employee, John was a theatrical old soul who would dress up everyday of the week just like a preacher going to church—dress pants, shirt, jacket, tie, and hat. But John only went to church on Sunday. The rest of the time, he was just on his way out to slop the hogs, stack the wood behind the huge kitchen stove, or tend to the other jobs Mrs. Cariker assigned him. It seemed to Mother that John was only partly concerned with appearances since he didn't go to any great pains to keep his fancy clothes clean. "John and Aunt Phein, the cook, used to yell at each other all the time," Mother said. "They seemed to have a continual battle about whether or not he could eat in the big house. Since Aunt Phein was so particular about her kitchen, she didn't want him trackin' up her clean floors. So, no matter what he wanted, he usually wound up eating outside."

Their arguments, though, were calm compared to those he frequently had with the assertive Mrs. Cariker. For some reason, John never quite realized that she was the boss. Now, everybody else recognized her position of authority, especially her mild-mannered husband, "Mr. Will." When Will got tired of following her orders, he would just simply curl up behind the big kitchen stove and take a nap. I guess that John's natural flamboyance and Mrs. Cariker's high-spiritedness just couldn't help but get cross-wired from time to time. Every week or so when he couldn't take it anymore, he would quit Mrs. Cariker and head on down to the Haynes Settlement to stay with some of his relatives. However, no one at the hotel took his departure too seriously because they all knew he would come back after a day or two. It seemed that when John was away from all the fussing at the hotel, his temper cooled and his flair for drama took on new dimensions. Most people who knew him remembered that he loved to sing and that he recited poetry with gusto. My friend, the late Lois Parker, told me that she had known him when she was a little girl and that he had a side job building the fires at the schoolhouse on cold mornings. The little children would eagerly gather around him because he would always come forth with such verses as:

Among the sand hills
Down by the sea,
Wild young rabbits
Were seen by me.

His presence seemed to entertain everybody he met, even Mrs. Cariker and Aunt Phein, although they never admitted it. He was certainly the bright spot in the day for all the sawmill workers when he would show up at noon with the lunches for those who stayed at the hotel. They knew he would be there because he was as predictable as the mill whistle. He had their lunches on time, and he always had something funny to say. No matter how many times they had heard it before, the men would roar when John yelled out right after the whistle blew, "It's 12 o'clock all over the world, all over the world!" And he was right; it was 12 o'clock all over *his* world!   During his off-duty hours, John was often seen hobbling down the road to visit friends. If Mrs. Cariker had made him mad or if a passerby yelled out and provoked him, he might pick up a stone or a rock and throw it at them. But most of the time, he would cheerfully call out to everyone he saw, "Hey, how ya' doin' today?" And when he was really happy, he would break out into a tune or two. The one that people remembered most was about the nearby town of Honey Island:

Honey Island, Honey Island
Come on and go with me.
Honey Island, Honey Island,
Is the place you long to be.

Cariker Hotel Recipes

 CHICKEN AND DUMPLINGS

Chicken and dumplings, a favorite boarding house dish, can be prepared several ways. Aunt Phein, Mrs. Cariker's first cook, often served this outstanding flat dumpling recipe.

1 large chicken
salt and pepper to taste

Place the seasoned chicken in a large pot, adding enough water to cover. Bring to a boil. Cover pot, reduce the heat, and simmer the chicken until tender. Remove the chicken from the broth and cool. Reserve the broth. Bone the chicken, cut the meat into pieces, and set aside.

 DUMPLINGS

1½ teaspoons salt
3 teaspoons baking powder
6 tablespoons butter, melted
1¼ cups sweet milk, room temperature
3¾ cups flour

Mix all ingredients in order listed and divide the dough in half. Roll half the dough very thin on a well-floured surface. Cut the dough into short strips. Set aside. Roll out and cut the remaining dough. Drop the dumpling strips into the boiling chicken broth. Cover, reduce heat, and simmer for approximately 40 minutes. Add chicken pieces the last 15 minutes. Add thickening to the broth if needed.

 SPICY ROAST

After Aunt Phein retired, Carrie Arline was the main cook at the hotel. Mrs. W. B. Mayo Cariker, Mrs. Cariker's daughter-in-law, told me that Carrie had a special way of cooking a roast. First, she would make small slits along the surface of the meat and place hot peppers in them, sometimes pouring a small amount of pepper juice into the slits. Next, she would salt, pepper, and flour the meat, then brown it in hot shortening in a heavy pot on top of the stove. Finally, she would add one or more cups of hot water to the pot, cover it, and place in a preheated 350° oven, cooking the meat until done.

This method makes the roast zesty and juicy.

AUNT PHEIN'S BREAD PUDDING

Of all the good food served at the Cariker Hotel, bread pudding was the one that my mother remembered most. Aunt Phein liked it because it was easy, Mrs. Cariker liked it because it was economical, and Mother liked it because it was delicious!

2 cups bread crumbs, toasted
1 pint cream or milk
½ cup sugar
½ cup butter, melted
4 eggs
pinch of salt
¼ teaspoon cinnamon
½ teaspoon vanilla
raisins (optional)

Soak bread crumbs in cream or milk. Mix sugar, butter, eggs, salt, and flavorings. Add to bread mixture. Pour into buttered baking dish. Bake at 350° for approximately 35 minutes.

 LEMON SAUCE

1 cup sugar
1 tablespoon flour
1 tablespoon butter
½ cup water
juice of 1 lemon

Mix all ingredients together and cook over low heat until thick. Serve warm over pudding.

The Honey Island Boarding House—after much of the excitement died down.
(*Courtesy Dorothy Childress.*)

THE HONEY ISLAND BOARDING HOUSE*

J ohn Foster wasn't the only person who had pleasant memories of Honey Island. My mother did too, and some of her favorite tales are woven from the memories of her life at the Honey Island Boarding House. Honey Island, one of the roughest early sawmill towns in the Big Thicket, was where she and my dad lived when they were newlyweds. Dad worked as a timekeeper at the mill, while Mother was principal, as well as teacher, at the high school. Until they could rent their own house, they lived at the Honey Island Boarding House, which my mother described as a primitive building with few amenities. She stayed there just long enough to realize that a distinctive feature of the place was its exotic wildlife.

One of the most annoying examples of that wildlife was an epidemic of bedbugs. It was on her first night there that she was introduced to the pesky little critters:

---

*With the exception of my parents Lester and Minnie Crews, Lester Holmes, and the Parker family, the names in this story have been changed—not to protect the guilty, but to protect me from the wrath of the guilty!

We'd already gone to bed that night when, all of a sudden, Lester got up and lit the kerosene lamp. We realized that we were being swarmed with bedbugs! Well, I began clawing and flicking those durned bugs off me as fast as I could. I thought, if this was what married life was all about, then I didn't want any part of it.

Although the problem of the bedbugs plagued my parents, it was fairly common in those days for people to have trouble with them. Only the most fastidious innkeepers kept them under control, and obviously the management at the Honey Island Boarding House was preoccupied with far different matters. One of the manager's most time-consuming concerns was her son. He was her only child, and he could do no wrong. Mother not only had to live under the same roof with him, but she also had to teach him. She and most of the other adults in town regarded him as being a generally obnoxious, foul-mouthed individual whose bad nature was compounded by the fact that he was named Dora. Later, whenever she heard the song about "a boy named Sue," she was instantly reminded of the trials she had endured at the hands of Dora.

Dora's hands got him and my mother into big trouble one day at school!

On this particular day, I kept hearing one of the girls in my class yell out from time to time. Finally, she came up to me and said that Dora, who sat in back of her, was putting a pin in his eraser and sticking it in her behind. Well, I told her to try to be calm and to go back and sit down and to let me handle the situation. I just quietly walked to the back of the room where I thought I could catch him in action. It didn't take long before he jabbed her again with that pin, and I rushed up there and paddled his hand really good. I didn't know it, but a little bit later, he went home and told his mamma what happened. I'm sure he forgot to tell her all the story. Later, when I was walking home to have lunch, I was surprised to see Mrs. Dennis, his mamma, come bounding out of the boarding house with a huge stick headin' my way. I wanted to run, but I knew if I did, I'd lose face with everybody in town, so I stood my ground. Well, you'd have thought there was about to be a shootout in Dodge City by the way everybody cleared the street. Why, even the mill foreman ran back into his house.

Anyway, Mrs. Dennis started screaming at me at the top of her lungs that I'd bruised her poor baby's hand and that she'd had to take him to the doctor. After a while, she quieted down enough for me to tell her the whole story. She was still mad when she left, but, thank goodness, she didn't hit me with that stick. I was too nervous to eat, so I decided to go over to the doctor's office and find out for myself if I really had hurt poor little Dora's hand. The doctor just died laughing when I asked him, and he told me not to worry a bit—that Dora's hand wasn't bruised—it was just dirty—and that he'd cleaned it with alcohol.

If Dora was a thorn in Mother's side, he was equally a pain in the tail-feathers of the parrot that lived at the boarding house. However, it wasn't Dora's dirty hands that caused the problem this time; it was his filthy mouth.

Now, as everybody knows, parrots are usually quick to imitate the words of the humans around them, so naturally, Dora's choice expressions were soon mimicked by the bird. One day, even Dora was embarrassed by the string of profanities that the bird blurted out in front of some of the boarders. So, to teach it a lesson, he jumped up, grabbed the bird, and ran outside to the nearest mud puddle. There, he rolled the bird over, dunked him in the mud, and scolded him repeatedly by saying, "Bad boy, bad boy." Then Dora put him on the backyard fence. It wasn't long before the old hog that'd been wallowing in another mud hole waddled alongside the fence. It's said that the bird looked down as the hog passed by, and just as if he saw the similarity of their plights, he called out, "Bad boy, bad boy!"

On another occasion, it was the parrot's whistling that got him into trouble, not his vocabulary. According to long-time resident Lester Holmes, the parrot caused a commotion at the boarding house and also throughout the town.

That parrot could talk; he could whistle; he could sing; he could do anything you could. Anyway, one day Andrew Robertson drove the wagon up there to deliver the groceries to the hotel, and he run right up by the side of the back fence and stopped his wagon and went in. That ol' parrot began to whistle and squawk out, "Git up, git up!" He had Andrew Robertson's voice down to a tee. He did this several times before those ol' mules got all feisty and, all of a sudden, started high tailin' it down the street with all them groceries still in the cart. Purty soon stuff started flyin' everywhere. I mean there were groceries all over the place.

After hearing that story, I decided I had heard enough about bedbugs, parrots, hogs, and bad boys. So, I set out to find an elderly black woman who had worked at the boarding house for years and who should have specific details. I drove to her house where I was not too well received by my prospective subject, who I will call Maybelle.

There were looks of surprise on her face as well as on the faces of her friends as I bounded out of my shiny new sedan and rushed up to them carrying my briefcase, my camera, and also my oversized tape recorder with its extended microphone. I should have at least introduced myself before invading their territory. "I'm looking for Maybelle who used to work at the Honey Island Boarding House," I said while turning on my recorder. After a long pause, all heads turned to one particular woman, but it took an even longer period of strained silence before she finally spoke. "I'se Maybelle, but I ain't never worked at no Honey Island Boarding House," she claimed. Again silence prevailed until at last, another woman declared, "Now, Maybelle, what are ya' talkin' 'bout? Ya' know ya' worked there!" At this point, Maybelle's eyes widened, and she shrieked unconvincingly, "What do ya' mean I'se worked there?" Then, more calmly, she answered, "Well, maybe I did, but I don't remember nuthin'. Nuthin' atall!"

No matter how I tried, I could not refresh her memory. Discouraged but not defeated, I finally decided to give up for the time being and to drive away to plan the strategy for my next encounter. Several hours later, I reappeared at Maybelle's house, this time bringing her current boss from the cafe, a man I will call Johnson. He had been really helpful in pointing out that the key to unlocking her faulty memory might have something to do with her love of fish. The minute I mentioned those big perch in my freezer, Maybelle's congeniality improved substantially and so did her memory.

I still didn't quite realize just what kind of story I was going to hear, but I soon found out that the activities at the Chicken Ranch* in La Grange were mild, boring, and somewhat puritanical compared to the wilder, more exciting and high-spirited times at the Honey Island Boarding House. The interview which followed, directed mainly by Johnson, got straight to the heart of the matter in no time flat.

> Johnson: Now, Maybelle, you ain't got around to tellin' me about all women there at the hotel. That's what I'm interested in is women.
>
> Maybelle: Yeah.
>
> Johnson: Well, how much did they charge, Maybelle?
>
> Maybelle: Oh, all the way from a dollar to seventy-five cents.
>
> Johnson: Would they stay with you all night or just a little while?
>
> Maybelle: Naw, when one'd leave, the other one would come in that's what they done.
>
> Johnson: Can you remember a funny story or two?
>
> Maybelle: I can remember one of 'em was called "'Lil Angel," and she was the out-dressinest woman I ever seen. She had more ol' men than the other women had, and them other women didn't like her. See, she was busy, real busy. I'd be upstairs cleanin' up, and she'd say, "Now, Maybelle, ya' got to be excused. I got business to tend to." I'd say, "Well, hell, tend to it!" Anyway, one night them other women

---

*A "house" notorious all over Texas for many years and made famous on Broadway by the musical comedy "Best Little Whorehouse in Texas."

jumped on 'Lil Angel. Good God Almighty, I'm tellin' ya' it was the biggest mess over there. 'Lil Angel would git put in jail, and they'd go git her out.

Johnson: Were they scratching and pulling hair?

Maybelle: Naw, Suh! Cuttin', they wus cuttin'. They'd use them ol' straight-handled razors. 'Lil Angel toted a razor all the time up under her dress in front a that brassiere. Nobody ever knew she had it in there till ya' messed with her.

Johnson: Well, did she stay there long?

Maybelle: She stayed there till that other lady, Miz Babin, took over. Miz Babin caught 'Lil Angel winkin' at her husband and tried to beat her up, but 'Lil Angel beat her up! Miz Babin told her if she didn't get outa there, she'd shoot her. I said, "Well, ya' let me git out first before ya' start shootin'! "Ohhhh, Lord, that's when I quit!

The fish were delivered to Maybelle's doorsteps early the next day.

After that surprising bit of news, I could now add the birds and the bees to my list of erratic and erotic wildlife stories. However, even with all this juicy information, I realized that I'd failed to locate any recipes. Surely, someone had time to cook amid all this confusion. It wasn't until months later when I interviewed the Parkers, one of the last families to manage the boarding house, that I discovered that indeed there was food and plenty of it, and that Mrs. Parker had written some of her favorite recipes in a spiral notebook. They told me that most of the excitement had died down by the time they took over in the '50s. Gone were the bedbugs, the bad boy, the parrot, the hog, and certainly the prostitutes. "But," one of them said, "let me tell you about this big ol' rat that lived between the walls and kept stealing everybody's soap and one day a boarder's false teeth even came up missin'. . . ."

"Thanks," I said, interrupting him as quickly as possible. "I'm only interested in recipes."

HONEY ISLAND BOARDING HOUSE RECIPES

Unlike the cooks of today who usually follow a written recipe, many of the early twentieth-century innkeepers filed their recipes somewhere in their heads. Therefore, at times it was difficult for me to duplicate their special dishes from simply hearing verbal instructions, which often included obscure measurements. Their telling me to "take a little bit of baking powder and sift it with a handful of flour; then take a scoop of sugar and cream it well with a lump of butter" caused me to produce a variety of inedible flops.

Fortunately, when the Parker family presented me with a spiral notebook filled with Mrs. Parker's basic recipes, I was delighted. The following recipes are from her collection and I highly recommend them all. Like the modern-day cook, I've made a written copy, but like the cooks of long ago, I've also filed these recipes away somewhere in my head.

 PEPPER RELISH

4 cups green pepper, chopped
4 cups sweet red pepper, chopped
4 cups onion, chopped
4 cups celery, chopped
1/4 cup salt
3 cups sugar
3 cups vinegar

Cover peppers, onion, and celery with boiling water. Drain after 5 minutes and add the rest of the ingredients. Boil rapidly for 10 minutes. Pour into sterilized jars and seal. (This is delicious when served over beans and peas.)

 MEAT LOAF

The pork and chili powder give this dish a special flavor.

1 lb. ground beef
½ lb. ground pork
1 onion, chopped
1 egg
1 teaspoon salt
2 teaspoons chili powder
3 slices bread
¼ cup milk

Mix meats, onion, egg, and seasonings thoroughly. Soak bread slices in milk and add to other ingredients. Shape into loaf and bake in oven at 350° for 1 hour.

 SPANISH RICE

4 tablespoons drippings
¾ cup onion, chopped
½ cup celery, chopped
½ cup green pepper, chopped
½ teaspoon salt
4 cups boiled rice
2 cups tomatoes, chopped
1 egg, beaten

Heat bacon drippings in a large frying pan. Add chopped onion and cook until lightly browned. Add celery, green pepper, and salt and cook for 5 minutes. Add cooked rice and chopped tomatoes and simmer for an additional 10 minutes. Stir in beaten egg and serve.

OATMEAL COOKIES

1 cup butter
2 cups sugar
2 eggs
1 teaspoon baking soda
1 teaspoon salt
1½ cups flour
1 teaspoon vanilla
3 cups oats

Cream butter and sugar. Add next 5 ingredients and beat well. Stir in oats. Chill. Drop on greased cookie sheet and bake at 325° about 10 minutes or until lightly browned. Add a small amount of flour to the dough if the first batch of cookies is too thin.

For a different taste, add 2 cups chopped pecans and 2 cups raisins.

DEVIL'S FOOD CAKE

1 cup unsifted, unsweetened cocoa
1 cup boiling water
2¾ cups sifted flour
1 teaspoon baking soda
½ teaspoon salt
1 teaspoon baking powder
1 cup butter, softened
2½ cups sugar
5 egg yolks, beaten well
1½ teaspoons vanilla
1 cup buttermilk
5 egg whites, beaten stiff

Combine cocoa with boiling water, mixing with a wire whisk until smooth. Cool completely. Sift flour with soda, salt, and baking powder. Grease well and flour four 8-inch layer cake pans. Preheat oven to 350°. With electric mixer, beat butter, sugar, egg yolks, and vanilla until light. Fold in flour mixture alternately with cocoa mixture and buttermilk. (Fold in only a small amount at a time.) Fold in beaten egg whites. Do not overbeat. Divide between pans and bake for 25 to 30 minutes. Cool in pans for 10 minutes, then remove from pans and cool completely on racks. Ice with seven-minute frosting.

SEVEN-MINUTE FROSTING

2 egg whites
1½ cups sugar
1½ teaspoons light corn syrup or ¼ teaspoon
  cream of tartar
⅓ cup cold water
dash of salt
1 teaspoon vanilla

Place all ingredients except vanilla in double boiler. Beat 1 minute with electric mixer. Cook over boiling water, beating constantly with mixer until peaks form, about 7 minutes. Remove from heat. Add vanilla. Beat until of spreading consistency. (For a chocolate seven-minute frosting, add 3 1-ounce squares unsweetened chocolate, melted and cooled, just before spreading on cake. Fold in and do not beat.)

LEMON CHESS PIE

1½ cups sugar
3 eggs
1 tablespoon flour
1 tablespoon cornmeal
6 tablespoons butter, melted
¼ cup lemon juice
¼ cup milk
⅛ teaspoon salt

Combine all ingredients and pour into an 8-inch unbaked pie shell. (See East Texas Hotel recipes for pie crust recipe, page 118.) Bake at 375° for 10 minutes. Reduce oven to 325° and bake for an additional 30 minutes.

OLD-FASHIONED FUDGE

3 cups sugar
½ cup cocoa
⅛ teaspoon salt
1½ cups milk
¼ cup butter
1 teaspoon vanilla

In a saucepan, combine sugar, cocoa, and salt. Place over a low heat and add milk gradually, stirring constantly until boiling point is reached. Cook to a soft ball stage without stirring (240°). (When tested in cold water, ball should flatten out when removed from water.) Add butter and vanilla. Don't stir. Cool to lukewarm (110°). Beat until creamy. Pour into a well-greased pan. Let cool completely.

The East Texas Hotel shortly before it was razed.

THE EAST TEXAS HOTEL

I n the northern part of the Big Thicket on Highway 69 lies the small town of Colmesneil. Named after W. T. Colmesneil, a well-liked passenger train conductor, the town was the junction for the Waco, Beaumont, Trinity, and Sabine Railroad and the Texas and New Orleans Railroad. Long-time resident Easter Matthews Mann, daughter of the last owners of the East Texas Hotel, Colmesneil's oldest, recalled that her parents awaited a T&NO telegram every morning telling them how many people wanted to eat lunch and what time to have it ready because the train only stopped for a few minutes. The other train, the WBTS, was affectionately known by the locals as the "Wobble, Bobble, Turn Around and Stop," an obvious nickname in view of the train's slow, precarious manner of shuffling down the tracks. In fact, according to Easter, the train was so slow that the passengers often had time to get off and pick flowers!

During its early days, Colmesneil was not the small town it is now. Believe it or not, it was actually larger than either Woodville (the Tyler County seat), or Beaumont. Ogden, the northern part of town, served as the main population and commercial center until the burning of the Yellow Pine Mill in 1893. This was the town's major business, and its destruction caused the population to shift southward.

There is still some question concerning the actual beginning dates of the town and the East Texas Hotel. Tyler County historian Lou Ella Moseley contends that both were established in 1882 with the coming of the railroad. Other sources project the date as being closer to the Civil War. A 1973 edition of the *Beaumont Enterprise* listed the date of the building of the hotel as being prior to 1876.

In that edition, Jim Andrews, a 107-year-old-native of Colmesneil, said that the East Texas Hotel was in existence the year he came from Kentucky as a nine-year-old boy. He recalled the hotel as being big and beautiful — "filled with fancy people and parties and good times." What an impressive sight the hotel must have been to the little boy "running alongside . . . [his] daddy's ox wagon." It was a sight he never forgot.

Although the East Texas Hotel closed in the 1940s, it still exerts a historical influence on another Southeast Texas restaurant. In 1973, Beaumont restauranteur Don Crain rescued some of the fixtures from the decaying hotel when he purchased the approximately 100-year-old building from the Matthews family and incorporated portions of it in Circa 100, his restaurant in Beaumont. He was intrigued by the beaded wall boards, the steep and narrow staircase with its slender balustrade, and the old oak doors with their porcelain knobs, and he hoped others would be also. As a result of his historical and artistic interests, he created a very elegant restaurant, which has since changed hands. It is now a popular night-spot and eating establishment called the Palace.

Throughout its lifetime, the hotel had several owners, but the Woodells were probably the most visible. Mrs. Moseley remembered hearing of the time Mrs. Woodell and several friends were sitting out on the front porch of the hotel discussing whether "the longer you live with a man, the more you love him or detest him." When questioned about her own lengthy marriage, Mrs. Woodell paused a minute and answered in her high-pitched little voice, "Well, I don't know about anybody else, but I like Evander *pretty* well!"

It was also during the Woodells' tenure at the East Texas Hotel that a general "knock-down-drag-out" took place. It resulted in a stabbing and a sustained rivalry between two local families due to differences of opinion concerning their business practices. In 1907, the Woodells

The lumber in the hotel was used in the Circa 100 Restaurant (now the Palace) in Beaumont.

and the Manns, owners of the Commercial Hotel, and their cohorts operated hotel/livery stable businesses. Each family hotly resented the other's intrusion into its territory. Mayo McBride, a long-time resident of Woodville, remembered that tempers flared when one of the Woodell boys had a fight with one of the older Manns at the depot and "kinda beat him up considerable and the Manns resented it considerable." McBride said that the whole thing got out of hand when Ferguson, an employee of the Manns, used a knife to repeatedly slash Joe Hill, the Woodells' son-in-law. Hill's father retaliated by taking the train to Woodville to buy an even bigger knife. Upon Hill's return, he surprised Ferguson, slit open his stomach, and then chased him around the train station until Dave Mann ordered him to stop. Because Ferguson was so badly hurt ("He was having to hold his entrails with his hand!") and because Hill refused to stop his assault, Mann shot and killed him. Mann was later acquitted by a jury in Woodville. Since the Manns outnumbered the Hills, the Manns suggested that the town wasn't big enough for both families and told them they were going to buy them out. The Hills sold out and moved away. More than eighty years later, though, hard feelings still exist between the two families.

Easter Mann remembered the East Texas Hotel as the site for more than just beddin' and boardin'. She recalled that the parlor sometimes served as a general meeting place for funeralizing as well as for socializing because at times the trains' unpredictable schedules made it necessary for the Matthews family to board the dead. Although it was hard on the nerves of the more squeamish tenants (warm bodies who didn't particularly relish the thought of spending the night so close to cold bodies), the occasional practice of boarding corpses did add variety to the general atmosphere of the hotel.

There were also problems associated with outdoor toilets, heat, and flies. One hot day, a traveling salesman indicated that he really needed to go to the privy, which stood behind the hotel, but he didn't want to because the flies were so bad. Another drummer chimed in, saying, "Oh well, if you'll just wait a few minutes, they'll have dinner on the table, and they'll all be in there!"

Speaking of dinner, Mrs. Mann remembered her mother's special technique for smoking hams. The secret to smoking delicious hams revolved around immersing them in dishpans of hot, soapy dishwater —a process her mother called "jerking" the ham. Then she hung them up and smoked them with hickory. "Of course," Mrs. Mann said, "it's more convenient to buy one at the supermarket now, but taste can't begin to compare." Although she enjoys the conveniences of today, Easter Mann will always have a soft spot in her heart for those by-gone hotel days. And anytime she feels too nostalgic for the East Texas Hotel, she can always go to the Palace in Beaumont. There, at least, she can soak up the atmosphere of the East Texas Hotel while enjoying a good meal, and she doesn't have to worry about the train pulling out . . . or the flies.

EAST TEXAS HOTEL
RECIPES

The term "pinching pennies" may not have been a coined expression in the early 1900s, but Big Thicket innkeepers had to be financially astute to realize any profit from their businesses. Meals in 1920 sold for around fifty cents each, so every penny, nickel, or dime saved was important.

Mr. Aaron Durham, a farmer near Colmesneil, knew that he was dealing with a clever businesswoman when he sold his produce to Savilla Matthews, the last proprietress of the East Texas Hotel. So, he devised a plan that was satisfactory to the both of them. He said, "I sold her lots of produce, especially peas, beans, chickens, and such as that. Now, if I wanted fifty cents for a chicken, I'd ask her sixty cents, 'cause I knew she'd talk me down a dime on any fryer or hen I'd take her."

It took more than Savilla Matthews' bargaining ingenuity to make ends meet, however. Careful planning and the hard work and cooperation of all the family members were also needed. "We made our own sausage and at times we even made hominy, sauerkraut, and sassafras tea," said Savilla's daughter, Easter Mann, remembering her busy days at the East Texas.

CHICKEN AND DRESSING

One of the specialities at the East Texas Hotel was chicken and dressing made by Totsy Bannister, an early cook. "It would be so moist and good," recalled Easter. "But see, Totsy didn't measure things. She just threw things together."

With Easter's help, I came up with the right combination of ingredients, and it's just as good as she said. Maybe one day I will feel confident enough to throw it together like Totsy did, but for now, I think I will just measure everything.

1 large hen, seasoned
water to cover
12 biscuits, baked
3 cups corn bread, crumbled
white bread, toasted and torn into small pieces
    (about 10 slices)
1½ cups onion, chopped
3 cups celery, chopped (celery tops included) *
¼ cup butter, melted
1 tablespoon sage
3 cups broth
2 eggs, beaten
salt and pepper to season

Season the hen generously with salt and pepper. Place the hen in a large pot, cover with water, cover the pot, and cook until tender. Reserve the broth and debone the chicken.

Crumble the bread into a large bowl. Sauté the onions and celery in butter until tender. Add to bread, along with sage, broth, beaten eggs, and salt and pepper to taste. Place the dressing in a greased baking dish and bake for approximately 30 minutes at 350°.

For moister dressing, use a smaller baking dish and pile the dressing higher. For a drier, crustier dressing, spread it in a longer dish.

---

*The celery was not included in the original recipe.

GIBLET GRAVY

neck, liver, and heart of chicken
5 cups water
salt and pepper to taste
⅓ cup butter
⅓ cup flour
2 eggs, hard-boiled and chopped

Place chicken pieces in the seasoned water and cook until tender. Remove chicken from broth and chop (excluding the neck). Set aside. In a pan, melt butter, add flour, and blend well. Stir in 3 cup of reserved broth. Cook until mixture thickens. Remove from heat and stir in chopped meat and chopped eggs. Serve hot over chicken and dressing.

HOMEMADE SAUSAGE

10 lbs. pork (8 lbs. lean meat and 2 lbs. fat meat)
20 feet of casings
⅓ cup salt
1 teaspoon sage
1 teaspoon chili powder

Place casings in water and soak for 30 minutes. Meanwhile grind pork in meat grinder. Add salt, sage, and chili powder and mix well. Remove casings from water and cut into desired lengths. Tie each section on one end. Slip the other end around the tapered part of a funnel and push the meat into the casing with your fingers. Squeeze along the length of the casing to push the meat down. Twist and tie casing.

COUNTRY-STYLE HOMINY

Few people around today know how to make hominy, so it is quickly becoming a lost art. But on the old-time farm, hominy making was a common practice.

In making hominy, hardwood ashes were saved in an ash hopper, which was actually a barrel or keg. The container, having a drain at the bottom, was placed on a low platform and tilted slightly. A pan was placed under the drain. After the ashes were packed into the container, water was added. The water would seep through the ashes and drain through the hole and into the pan. The liquid, called potash, was a strong solution of lye and was a deep red in color.

The liquid was poured into a wash pot, large-grain corn was added, a fire was built, and the corn was cooked until the skin came off. The corn was then removed from the pot and washed until all the husks came off and all the lye was removed. Finally, the corn kernels, which were bleached white and fluffy, were stored in large containers until they were cooked.

FRIED HOMINY

¼ cup bacon drippings
3 cups hominy
salt and pepper to taste

Heat the bacon drippings in a skillet. Add the hominy and fry over a low heat, stirring gently until lightly brown. Add salt and pepper.

SAUERKRAUT

Remove outside leaves and core from firm heads of cabbages. Weigh up 5 pounds. Wash well and shred very fine. Mix 3½ tablespoons of salt with the shreds, using hands.

Put mixture very gently into a crock and press it down. Cover with a cloth. Put a plate over the cloth and put a "sad-iron" (a heavy flat-iron) in the plate for a weight. Skim daily to remove the scum as it rises. The kraut will "make" in ten to twelve days. Taste it and if it is tender, it is cured.

Pack solidly in sterilized jars, leaving about ½ inch at the top of the jar. Add kraut juice to cover. If there is not enough brine, make more, using 2 tablespoons of salt to 1 quart of water.

Cap and seal. Process jars in boiling water for 15 minutes.

 SOUTHERN PECAN PIE

Filling:
>   4 eggs, slightly beaten
>   1 cup sugar
>   1 cup light corn syrup
>   ¼ cup butter
>   2 teaspoons vanilla
>   1 cup pecans, coarsely chopped

Cream eggs and sugar. Add syrup, butter, and vanilla and blend well. Stir in pecans. Pour mixture in a 9-inch unbaked pie shell and bake at 350° for 1 hour. When crust browns after approximately 45 minutes, you may want to cover the pie loosely with foil to prevent further browning.

Pie Crust:
>   1⅓ cups flour
>   ½ teaspoon salt
>   ½ cup shortening
>   3 tablespoons tap water

Sift flour and salt together. Cut in shortening until it resembles coarse cornmeal. Sprinkle water over mixture, a little at a time, and blend well. Roll dough in a circle and place in pie plate. Double recipe to make 2 pie crusts.

INDIAN PUDDING

4 cups milk
⅔ cup Indian meal (or any other kind of
  coarse cornmeal)
1 egg, slightly beaten
½ cup molasses
¾ teaspoon salt
1 teaspoon ginger
1 cup raisins
¼ cup butter, melted

Scald milk. Pour milk slowly into meal, stirring constantly. Pour mixture into top of a double boiler and cook over medium heat for 20 minutes, stirring frequently. Remove from heat and add egg, molasses, salt, ginger, and raisins. Stir well and pour into a buttered pan. Bake for 45 minutes at 325°. Pour butter over pudding and continue baking for 15 minutes. Serve warm with whipped cream or ice cream.

GINGERBREAD WITH RAISIN CREAM SAUCE

1 cup butter
1½ cups sugar
5 eggs, beaten
1 cup pure cane syrup
1 cup molasses
3 cups flour, sifted
2 teaspoons ginger
1 teaspoon soda
1 teaspoon cinnamon
¼ teaspoon salt
1 teaspoon soda dissolved in ½ cup milk

Cream butter and sugar. Add eggs, syrup, and molasses, and mix well. Add dry ingredients and milk alternately. Pour into a greased and floured baking pan and bake at 350° for approximately 35 minutes. Serve warm with raisin cream sauce.

Raisin Cream Sauce:
⅓ cup butter
6 tablespoons flour
½ cup sugar
¼ teaspoon salt
3 cups milk
½ teaspoon nutmeg
1 cup raisins

In saucepan, melt butter and stir in flour, sugar, salt, and milk. Cook slowly until mixture thickens, stirring constantly. Remove from heat and stir in nutmeg and raisins.

 SASSAFRAS TEA

Years ago people drank sassafras tea because of the curative powers they believed it possessed. Particularly in the spring of the year mothers gave it to their children as a tonic to thin their blood.

    6 – 2-inch roots of sassafras
    6 cups water

Place sassafras roots in a saucepan. Pour water over the roots and bring to a boil slowly. Remove from heat. Cover and let steep until desired strength. Strain and serve with sugar, sugar and cream, or as is.

Main Street—Batson, 1904. (*Courtesy Mrs. Eda Ammans Johnson.*)

The Caledonia/ Aunt Doll's Boarding House

A lthough the timber industry dominated the economic scene of the Big Thicket in the late nineteenth century, oil played a significant role in the wealth of the area during the early years of the twentieth. In Batson, Saratoga, and Sour Lake, the "get-rich-quick" crowd blew in just about as soon as the wells did, and before anybody knew what had happened, these sleepy little communities were transformed into three of the wildest boom towns in Texas. From all accounts, Batson had the other two beaten, and if violence could have been gauged then on the Richter scale of one to ten, Batson would have surely rated an eleven.

Batson's inaccessible locale may have been a prime reason for the lawlessness which prevailed there. It was miles away from any other town or railroad, and since the corduroy roads into town "would shake you plumb to death," many people chose to walk, or sometimes wade, rather than ride.

Once, when a gambler was asked by a saloon-keeper what he thought of the town he replied, "Well, while I might not accuse everybody

here of being a crook, I'd say that every crook who can get here is here!"

Minnie West, who moved to Batson at the height of the boom in 1904, recalled that the main street, Fannin Street, "wasn't fit for any decent man, woman, child, or beast,":

> Crude buildings, which were mostly saloons were thrown up on each
> side of that ol' muddy road with boardwalks for people to walk on.
> Tents were everywhere — between and behind the buildings where lots
> of people lived. You see, nobody could have their own place 'cause the
> oil companies owned the land. They had to pay a ground rent and this
> caused one or two of the fellers to build their places up in trees. I
> remember even the law had a sort of tree house back behind ol' Black
> Cat Jim's place so they could watch all the goings-on down the street.
> It was terrible—all the shootin', killin', and stuff.

Mrs. West remembered that, at first, there were several boarding houses to accommodate the large crowds, but when the boom was over so was the big demand for room and board, and the only one to remain was the Caledonia. Although the Hawkinses and the Starks were the first to run it, in 1913 her cousin Eda's folks, the Ammans, took over, and she imagines that "Eda and I are probably the only ones around here now who can still remember how bad things were."

When I visited with Eda Ammans Johnson, she agreed with her cousin Minnie on the despicable conditions of the town:

> It was a hell-hole then, and if anybody would've told me I was going
> to spend the rest of my life here, I'd have told them they were crazy.
> And to think we had to go to all sorts of trouble to get there. Why, it
> took us all day to come the six miles from Saratoga where we got off
> the train. See, it was raining real hard and all we had was our coats.
> So, before we started, we had to go up town and buy some tablecloths
> — oil-cloths — that's all we could get to spread over us. In the wagon,
> they brought chairs for us to sit in, and you couldn't hardly stay in
> them. The road would get so bad from time to time until we'd leave it
> and just make another road. There wasn't no bridge over the bayou

Some people built
their houses up in
trees to keep from
paying a ground
rent—Batson, 1904.
(*Courtesy Mrs. Eda
Ammans Johnson.*)

down there. We had to go right on through it. When we finally got
here, there wasn't no place to stay, so when Mother was offered the
job of running the Caledonia, we moved in there. It was right out in
the middle of the oil field where the water from the wells stood all the
time. You couldn't go out without rubber boots, and the mosquitoes
were something awful. One time, they got so bad that they started
killing the cattle. They'd get up in their noses and smother them. We
had to build smokes all around the yard to keep them off. We'd have
to rake up lots of cow chips and put them into piles and then pour
kerosene on them.

So, with a crust of cow manure (which incidently didn't blaze but instead emitted a thick, foul-smelling cloud of smoke for hours), unbearable heat with no air-conditioning, and a few hundred thousand hearty mosquitoes that were not only *not* repelled by the smoke but seemed to thrive on it, life in the summer must have been torture for the boarders.

Unpleasant memories are often dimmed with the passing of time, but Mrs. Johnson could forget her own name about as easily as she could forget those endless hours of backbreaking work required to care for the boarders:

> The sheets and bedcovers would be just covered with oil and grease, and we'd have to beat them for the longest time in a pot of boiling soapy water, but, thank goodness, we didn't have to wash their grimy clothes. The boarders took care of that themselves by taking their clothes out to the oil field and washing them in wash boxes. The boxes had hooks on them, and they could be hung upon shacklelines, which were the lines which connected the wells to the big bull wheel in the pump room. The boxes had boards nailed on the bottom so that when the shacklelines went back and forth, the clothes would be agitated just like a washing machine.
>
> Of course, not all the boarders were oil field workers. One of the funniest was an old preacher who could hardly get around. He'd just sit there moanin' and groanin' with his rheumatism, havin' everybody wait on him hand and foot while he preached a sermon or two on the mysterious ways the Lord moved. Once, during a stormy season, we got a chance to see those mysterious ways for ourselves. The first time a storm came through, that old preacher just sat there while everybody had to struggle to carry him to a safer place. It took us forever to get him moved. But, I'm tellin' you, the next time we heard about one coming, he outran us all . . . He plum forgot all about that rheumatism tryin' to get away.
>
> We were so glad to leave that place that we sold everything . . . furniture, dishes, and pots. The only thing I got was a toothpick holder.

Although the Ammans family did not find their true calling to be running a boarding house, the next proprietor did. Lavinia Davis

Larche, otherwise known as Aunt Doll, really did find hotel keeping to be her avocation as well as her vocation. Old-timers remembered her as being a big jovial high-spirited woman, with an even bigger heart, who exerted a positive influence on everyone around her.

Nobody's quite sure of when Aunt Doll appeared on the scene or how she got her nickname, but it was as if the folks of Batson woke up one day and there she was, establishing a name for herself as a truly talented and energetic humanitarian hotel-keeper. Walter McCreight, a resident of the town, said, "She could reach out to others with her own special brand of humanity. One of the highlights of her life was helpin' others to eat good food . . . keepin' everybody happy that way."

I don't know if the way to a man's heart actually is through his stomach, but Aunt Doll's good cooking obviously must have helped her matrimonial plans. Soon after she moved to Batson in the early '20s, she married one of her boarders, Lafayette "Fete" Caruthers. Walter McCreight recalled that the whole town turned out for the wedding supper at the hotel after the marriage. At the party, the crowd gathered around for an old-fashioned shivaree* and watched delightedly as the men hauled Fete into the woods.

It was during the Depression years that Aunt Doll's benevolence became most apparent. Although she knew that she couldn't feed the world, she did her best to feed the hungry people in Batson. Jude Hart, a native of the area, said that sometimes there would be as many as sixty people standing at Aunt Doll's back door, waiting for food:

> Whether you had money or not, she would always take 'em in and feed 'em. She'd say, "Well, ya'll just get out and hustle some smoke wood." They'd go to the woods and pack in ol' rotten wood. Like the cow chips, that was good to make smoke . . . . She'd give 'em odd jobs to do, ya' know, to make 'em feel better.

---

*It was the custom at many French weddings for the men to "kidnap" the bridegroom and take him to a remote place where he was left alone with only his own resources to find his way back.

I thought a while back that Aunt Doll's place should've been named the "Honeymoon Hotel" 'cause when all these ol' boys around here got married, they'd go up there and get 'em a room and spend their honeymoon there . . . She'd always let 'em; she always seemed to manage it.

But her big-heartedness and romantic nature finally got her into big trouble with Fete. After a while, he'd had all that he could take of her generous participation in the lives of countless others, so he left her. Batson resident Buck Hobbs remembered the day the divorce papers were served. The prospect of delivering the papers caused lots of speculation as to whether or not she'd actually sign them, and Fete indicated that he was pretty sure she wouldn't. She surprised everyone by signing as she said, "Well, if that's what he wants, then that's what he's gonna get." When the constable who delivered them returned to present the completed documents, Fete said, "Uh, huh. She wouldn't sign 'em would she? I told you so!" Imagine his reaction when he found out that they were signed, sealed, and delivered. Aunt Doll had the last laugh because Fete soon found that a divorce was not what he really wanted, and they were remarried shortly thereafter.

Ethel Richey McCreight was sixteen when she moved to Batson in 1930 to live with her Uncle Fete and Aunt Doll. As a member of a large family which was experiencing hard times during the Depression, Ethel, wanting to be an asset rather than a liability, knew that she was always welcome at her relatives' boarding house. And what an asset she was! In addition to being "sweet sixteen," she could help with the cooking, she could sing and yodel, and she could play a guitar. According to Ethel:

> Aunt Doll was big and heavy on her feet, so she would sit in a big lattice-back straight chair at the kitchen table and C. B., the colored boy, and I would hand her whatever she wanted. She'd actually do all the cooking, though. We'd just do things like whip the egg whites, wash dishes, stir the pots, and anything else she had for us to do.
>
> Every night, the ones that stayed there wanted me to sing certain different ol' songs. They'd all sit there in the dining room after dinner,

Aunt Doll's Boarding House—early 1930s. The girl standing to the right of the building is Ethel Richey. *(Courtesy Ethel Richey McCreight.)*

and I'd pick my guitar and sing. You see, my mother was a Caruthers and all the Caruthers were pretty musical. Jimmie Rodgers songs, such as "T for Texas, T for Tennessee," were popular then and a lot of times I'd yodel. I thought I was doing good 'cause sometimes they'd pitch some money out, you know. Well, the music would just might near get in my feet.

One song that I sung a lot was "Seven Years with the Wrong Woman."

> Seven years with the wrong woman
> will wreck most any good man.
> Seven years with the wrong woman
> is more than a man can stand.
> Seven years with the wrong woman
> will drive most any man bad.

All you can do is dig you a hole
and pull the ground over you.

Aunt Doll was of French descent and learned to cook in the typical French fashion, which meant slow cooking and careful watching. Like many other French cooks, she believed that all fresh vegetables should be wilted or steamed first in bacon drippings. If water was needed, it was later added and the food simmered until done.

Aunt Doll continued to run the hotel off and on until she got too old to manage it. Then in about 1938 she and Fete moved to their own private residence.

Although Eda Johnson still lives in Batson, she no longer calls it a hell-hole; she calls it a hole-in-the-road instead. Anyone who drives through today will understand what she means. Compared to the boom town it was in 1904, it is practically a ghost town now. It takes a vivid imagination to believe that there were once over 10,000 people when there are so few now.

THE CALEDONIA
RECIPES

Probably the most frequently prepared dessert at any boarding house was the basic One-Two-Three-Four Cake. It could be baked in layers and iced; it could be cooked as a pound cake and topped with fresh fruit, preserves, or different sauces; it could be converted to tea cakes by simply omitting the milk.

I never realized that the cake and cookie recipes were so similar until Mrs. Eda Johnson told me.

 ## ONE-TWO-THREE-FOUR CAKE

1 cup butter
2 cups sugar
1/4 teaspoon salt
4 eggs, separated
3 cups flour, sifted before measuring
3 teaspoons baking powder
1 cup milk
2 teaspoons vanilla

Preheat oven to 375°. Cream butter, sugar, and salt together until light and fluffy. Add beaten egg yolks and blend until smooth. Sift flour and baking powder together and add to first mixture along with milk and vanilla. Beat egg whites until stiff and fold into mixture. Pour batter into three 8-inch round cake pans or two 9-inch pans. Bake for 35 to 40 minutes. Ice with Seven-Minute-Frosting or Jam Cake Icing. (See page 105 for frosting recipe.) (See page 9 for icing recipe.)

OLD-FASHIONED TEA CAKES

1 cup butter
2 cups sugar
¼ teaspoon salt
4 eggs
3 cups flour, sifted before measuring
3 teaspoons baking powder
2 teaspoons vanilla

Preheat oven to 375°. Cream butter, sugar, and salt together until light and fluffy. Add beaten eggs and blend until smooth. Sift flour and baking powder together and add to first mixture. Stir in vanilla. Chill dough for easier handling. Divide dough into four parts. Place each part on separate sheets of lightly floured wax paper. Roll into rolls and slice. Bake on ungreased cookie sheet for approximately 12 minutes.

AUNT DOLL'S BOARDING HOUSE RECIPES

 FRIED CHICKEN

Aunt Doll always put her chicken in cold milk and let it set there. Then she'd season it and fry it in grease that was just the right temperature. It'd make a lot of crunch.

— *Ethel Richey McCreight*

1 fryer, cut up
cold milk (enough to soak chicken pieces)
salt and pepper to season
2 cups flour
shortening for frying

Soak chicken in cold milk for several hours. Remove chicken, season with salt and pepper and dredge in flour. Place pieces in hot shortening and quickly brown them on both sides. Turn the heat down to medium temperature and continue cooking, turning frequently, until chicken is done. Serve with cream gravy. (See page 81 for cream gravy recipe.)

 FRIED FROG LEGS

One time, Aunt Doll bought a whole bunch of bull frogs, and I had never cooked any before. I put 'em in that hot grease and when they started to jumpin', I got scared. I thought they wasn't dead. Aunt Doll started laughing, and I said, "Aunt Doll, they look too much like babies bendin' over, like babies' hinies stickin' up."
— *Ethel Richey McCreight*

> frog legs
> salty vinegar water
> salt and pepper to season
> flour
> shortening for frying

Clean frog legs and soak them overnight in a cold salty vinegar water solution. Remove from water, dry off with a clean cloth, season with salt and pepper, and dredge in flour. Fry in hot grease until brown, lower temperature slightly, and continue cooking until done.

CREAMED STEWED ONIONS

15 small boiling onions
salt and pepper to taste
¼ cup bacon drippings
white sauce

Season onions with salt and pepper and place in pot. Add bacon drippings. Simmer until tender and cover with white sauce. (See page 55 for white sauce recipe.)

BAKED SWEET POTATOES

5 or 6 average size sweet potatoes
salt
1 cup water
1 cup brown sugar
1 cup sugar
½ cup butter
1 teaspoon cinnamon
1 teaspoon nutmeg

Peel and cut uncooked potatoes in lengthwise sections. Layer 2 potatoes deep in long buttered baking pan. Salt potatoes lightly and add ½ cup water. Cover pan, place in 350° oven, and cook potatoes until partly tender. In the meantime, heat sugars and ½ cup water, making a syrup. Uncover baking pan, dot potatoes with butter, sprinkle with spices and pour in syrup. Lower temperature to 300°, cover pan, and continue baking until potatoes are completely tender, basting often. Uncover, raise temperature to 375°, and brown potatoes slightly.

 BERRY COBBLER

3 quarts fresh dewberries or blackberries
1½ cups water
1 cup sugar
pie crust for 2 pies
½ cup flour
½ cup sugar
butter

Bring berries, water, and 1 cup sugar to a boil. Turn down heat and cook gently for 10 minutes. While the berries are cooking, make pie crust dough for 2 pies. (See East Texas Hotel recipes, page 118, for double pie crust recipe.) Divide dough, cutting half of dough into long strips. Roll out other half of dough to fit 9 x 13 baking dish. Set aside. Grease dish and pour in half of cooked berries. Mix ½ cup flour and ½ cup sugar together and sprinkle half of the mixture over the berries. Place browned dough strips (lattice style) over berries and dot with butter. Repeat with remaining berries and flour and sugar mixture. Top with unbaked dough and dot with pats of butter. Bake in oven at 350° for approximately 1 hour.

The Vines Hotel. (*Courtesy Big Thicket Museum.*)

THE VINES HOTEL

As a little girl, one of my favorite things to do was to go camping with my family on Village Creek in the Big Thicket. I would always get so excited just thinking about it that I could hardly sleep a wink for days before we left. We did this every year until I was about eleven and then, for some reason, my mother decided that this was one experience she could live without and stopped going. After that, it was never quite as much fun for my sister and me because we had to take over all Mother's duties as chief cook and pot scrubber. But up until then, it was sheer delight to swim and fish in the creek, pick all kinds of wild flowers, and sleep out under the stars at night. Although as an adult I have taken some wonderful trips to distant and exotic places and spent lots of money traveling, I don't think anything can compare to the fun that I used to have camping out in the piney woods.

My dad believed in traveling light, so usually all we took was a tarpaulin, some old quilts, a few pots and pans, and very little food. (Maybe this was why Mother quit going!) Dad prided himself in being "the Great White Hunter" and generally was successful in supplying us with all the fish and squirrels we could eat. He and I would get up at the crack of dawn and row out into the eerie fog, eager to see what we had caught on the trotlines we had set the night before. Sounds of

Inside the Vines Hotel. (*Courtesy Big Thicket Museum.*)

nature were all around us. The spooky noises of an owl screeching and a panther screaming, mingled with the merry chirps of the crickets and birds and the constant croaking of the multitude of frogs, formed a kind of eclectic chorus. Naturally, I did not realize then what a diversified habitat we were visiting, but I am sure my childhood interest contributed greatly to the interest that I now have in the flora and fauna of the region.

Variety is the spice of life in the Thicket. While there are countless species of plants and animals, there are just about as many varieties of people there. Oh, sure, I had always known that I had some pretty "fascinating" relatives, but what I had not known was eccentricity was the universal Big Thicket trait. Most people there are not pretentious, and they could care less about keeping up with the Joneses—even if there were any Joneses to keep up with. I do not know what is in the

Mattie Evans. *(Courtesy Elmo Rosier.)*

woods that seems to nurture that lust for individuality. Maybe it's something in the air or in the drinking water, but whatever it is, everybody seems to march to the beat of his own little drummer.

Two people who exemplified the "Big Thicket Personality" were Mattie "Aunt Matt" Evans, the owner of the old Vines Hotel in

Mattie and her first husband, Lee Naney, 1903. (*Courtesy Elmo Rosier.*)

Saratoga, and her nephew, Lance Rosier, a naturalist who had grown up in the hotel and later became known as "Mr. Big Thicket." Of course, they did not have to try to be colorful; they were just naturally that way.

Elmo Rosier, Aunt Matt's great-nephew, turned out to be one of my best resources on Aunt Matt and Lance. Because Elmo had spent so much time at the hotel as a little boy, he probably knew the pair better than anybody else, and he had inherited an old trunk containing their keepsakes and valued possessions. For some reason, he had never gone through the trunk himself but was happy to help me look through it. We first found hand-written family deeds dating back to 1852, but as we dug deeper, even more of Aunt Matt's history began to unfold.

Aunt Matt was one of several children of Thomas C. Jordan, a prominent landowner who had come to the Big Thicket in the 1840s from Alabama. During the early years of this century, when oil was discovered in Saratoga, Jordan offered each of his children 100 acres

Mattie and her second husband, Bobby Evans.
(*Courtesy Big Thicket Museum.*)

of prime timberland. Mattie, who had just recently married, must have
been more intrigued by the hustle and bustle of life in the boom town
than she was by the prospect of a more socially sedentary life on a
farm, because she talked her father into building her a hotel instead
of giving her the land. No one seems to remember what the hotel was
called at first, but it soon became known as the Vines because of the
massive English Ivy which completely covered one side of the building.
"Some people seemed to think that the vine was the only thing holding
up the hotel," Elmo laughed. Whether due to good construction or
the English Ivy, the Vines lasted until the 1960s.

In the hotel's early years, Aunt Matt did a booming business by
providing good meals and a home for many of the oil field workers.
In fact one of the boarders, Bobby Evans, was so comfortable that he

decided he would stay on forever, and he wound up marrying Mattie in 1908. Mattie's marriage to Evans, who was one of the early leaders in the oil workers' union, was happy and enduring. While they never had children of their own, they provided a home for several nieces and nephews.

Elmo told me that, like so many people in the Thicket, Aunt Mattie was pretty close-mouthed and considered her affairs her own business:

I suppose between my great-aunt Matt and my Uncle Lance, I knew more about their business than anybody else, and that wasn't much. One thing they'd never tell you was their age. Aunt Matt would always laugh and say, "Oh, I'm old enough to sleep by myself," while Lance's reply was, "I'm past 62." Of course, he never told you how much past 62 he was.

According to Elmo, Lance Rosier loved his outdoor surroundings and spent his entire life studying nature. Even as a small boy, he would wander through the woods and nearby savannahs admiring the trees and wild flowers of the Thicket and learning their scientific as well as their common names. While others abused the habitat by cutting the timber and killing off the wild game, he quietly began advocating the protection of it. The Big Thicket was his first love, and he fought for it all of his life. As he grew older, many people thought it was strange indeed that he did not go out and get a real job but chose instead to roam through the woods. What the people did not know was that in reality he was on the payroll of three oil companies. "If they wanted to know anything about their land or land boundaries, they could always count on Lance for the answers," Elmo recalled.

With the development of the conservation movement in the 1930s, more and more scientists heard about the self-taught naturalist of the Big Thicket and sought his services. By then, the boom in Saratoga was over, the hotel clientele had dwindled, and the Vines began to function primarily as the headquarters for Lance's guide business. Elmo recalled:

Big Thicket naturalist Lance Rosier.
(*Courtesy Big Thicket Museum.*)

A bunch of botanists and their students came down from some college, and Lance took them out. By lunch, Lance had had enough talkin' and was ready for some peace and quiet while he ate his sweet potato and some bacon, so he goes over and sets down on a log by himself. Well, they got to talking 'bout a plant that they found that they didn't know the name of and finally decided that they'd have to go back and key it out. After a while, one of the ladies in the group passed by Lance to git a drink of water from a jug settin' by him. He looked up and told her quietly, "I know what the name of that is, I know what the Latin name is, and I know what the common name is." Well, she goes back and tells the group, and Lance said that they all looked at him just like a bunch of chickens lookin' at a snake. So whenever they got back there and keyed it out, it sure 'nuff was what he'd said. Then, whenever this doctor asked him how many different kinds of plants could he identify, he said, "Well, somethin' like 300."

Later, particularly during the time that conservationists were pushing for the Big Thicket National Preserve in the '60s and early '70s, Lance conducted many distinguished visitors, including Secretary of the Department of the Interior Stewart Udall and Supreme Court Justice William O. Douglas, through the Thicket and was on a first name basis with United States Senator Ralph Yarborough. In addition, he was awarded several honorary degrees, became the thirty-ninth member of the National Academy of Sciences, and was written about in national publications. This was quite a list of accomplishments for someone who had often been criticized for not getting a real job.

Vines Hotel
Recipes

 HOG KILLIN' DAY

Years ago, each fall when the first norther blew into East Texas, the jig was up for many a backyard rooter. Rural folks like Aunt Matt decided that "Porky" had been piggin' out long enough on things like corn and watermelon, and the weather was just right to help preserve his parts until they made it to the smoke house or to the dinner table. Since pork was the main source of meat for most country residents during the winter months, it was important that the hog's last rites be properly executed. The ritual, long and tedious, started early in the morning and lasted well into the day.

First, someone filled the cast iron wash pot with water and heated it while someone else cornered the rooter, tied him, and went for the jugular. Then, when the water reached the scalding point, it was poured into a vat or barrel in preparation for the animal's final—probably only—bath.

The saying, "You got the right scald," a saying I've heard all my life meaning the food has been seasoned properly, must have originated on hog killin' day because it was necessary that the water be scalding but not boiling. If the water was too cold, it would not loosen the hair; if it was too hot, it would set it. At any rate, when everyone agreed on the water conditions, the hog was immersed head first into the water and twirled around by his feet until his hair began to slip. When this happened, he was pulled out, turned over, and dipped into the water in reverse. Generally, more hot water had to be added at this point. Next, the carcass was removed from the water, placed on boards, and the scraping process was begun. This procedure had to be done very quickly before the hair set. When the hair was scraped, the animal resembled a baby's bottom, pink and soft. But he was not pretty for long because his hind legs were soon attached to a singletree (the wooden cross-bar used at the front of a wagon or plow) and he was hoisted up to a tree limb or scaffold where the singletree was attached. Finally, the carcass was disemboweled and dismembered.

People tended not to be wasteful back in the early days—especially when it came to making the most out of a hog. It seems to me that the only thing that escaped was his squeal. While the hams, loins, shoulders, and middlings (side meat) were cured and smoked, the other parts were utilized in every possible fashion.

Although the number of pork dishes are not as common today as they were back then, they are still enjoyed by some. For this reason, I collected the following recipes from Elmo Rosier, Aunt Matt's great-nephew, and various boarding house people. I had originally planned to test all the pork recipes, but when I used chitlins instead of cracklins and ruined the corn bread, I decided to give it up.

I have never understood why hog parts are not all called by their right names. I think it was to fool the kids. But I guess it did sound better to say, "Let's eat some chitlins," rather than, "Why don't we fry up some intestines."

PRESERVING PORK

By curing and smoking the choice sections of the hog, they could be preserved throughout the winter months.

First, the meat was laid on a shelf and rubbed with a curing solution. A good basic solution (for 100 pounds of meat) would consist of the following ingredients:

> 8 lbs. pure salt (not iodized)
> 2½ lbs. brown sugar (heated)
> 2 oz. saltpeter
> 2 oz. black pepper
> 2 oz. red pepper

Then, the meat would be packed away in a barrel or a box. After a few days, the meat was removed, checked (to see that all parts had made contact with the curing solution), and repacked (heavier pieces on bottom) until the curing procedure was complete. Generally, it would take two days for each 1 pound of meat. (For example, a 10 pound ham would take twenty days.) After the meat was cured, the solution was either wiped off or washed off, and the individual pieces were usually put in cloth sacks or wrapped in some type of cloth.

Next, the meat was hung from rafters in the smokehouse and smoked. To smoke the meat, ashes were put in the bottom of a big can or bucket, pieces of wood (preferably hickory) were placed in the container, and a fire was started. As soon as there was a good fire, a lid (with holes) was placed on the container. When the lid was put on, the fire was smothered out, and the smoking process began. The meat was smoked for approximately a week or until it turned light brown. The smokehouse was closed to keep the smoke inside. Usually, the meat was allowed to set for several days before any of it was eaten.

PORK RECIPES
(FROM HEAD TO TOE!)

 HOG'S HEAD CHEESE

1 head
4 feet
4 hocks
1 tongue
1 heart
1½ lbs. liver
fat pork meat
5 large onions, chopped
4 cups green onions, chopped
salt and red pepper to taste

Scald, clean, and scrape head and feet thoroughly. Place in large pot, along with hocks, tongue, heart, liver, and pork meat. Cover with water and boil. Skim off foam that rises to the top, add large onions, and continue cooking until meat falls off bones. Remove fat that has settled on top. Remove meat from stock and reserve stock. Debone and run meat through food grinder. Season meat with salt and pepper. Put meat into pot with stock. Add green onions. Let cook over low heat until mixture begins to jell. Pour into ungreased pans, press with weight, and chill overnight.

 BRAINS AND EGGS

Boil brains until tender. Remove skin and cut into pieces. Cook in butter until done. Add 4 or more well-beaten eggs and continue cooking until eggs are done. Season to taste with salt and pepper.

LIVER AND LIGHTS (LUNGS)

Cut liver and lights into small pieces. Cover with cold water. Add 1 chopped onion and salt to season. Simmer for approximately 2½ hours.

Serve with sweet potatoes, greens, and corn bread.

 ## FRIED SALT PORK

1–3 lb. lean whole salt pork shoulder
2 tablespoons cooking oil
pepper to taste

Cook salt pork in boiling water until tender. Slice the pork into desired thickness. Fry in the oil slowly until slightly brown. Serve with cream gravy. (See Scott Hotel recipes, page 81.)

 ## CRACKLINGS

Cracklings, the crisp brown pieces of pork remaining after lard is rendered, can be eaten by themselves, but are also good when added to corn bread recipes.

5 lbs. fresh pork fat, cubed
2½ cups water

Put pork pieces and water in a large pot, heat water to boiling, reduce heat, cover pot, and simmer until water has cooked away. Remove the lid; raise the temperature slightly, continue cooking, and stir frequently (and carefully). It should take approximately 45 minutes for the meat to brown. If the grease begins to brown, reduce the heat. Remove fat pieces and drain.

CRACKLING CORN BREAD

¼ cup shortening
2 cups cornmeal
1 teaspoon salt
1 teaspoon baking soda
1 cup cracklings (Crisp bits of bacon can be substituted
    for cracklings, if desired.)
2 cups buttermilk
2 eggs, beaten

Preheat oven to 425°. Heat the shortening in an iron skillet in oven. Mix the cornmeal, salt, baking soda, and cracklings. Stir in the buttermilk. Add well-beaten eggs to the batter. Stir in the melted shortening from the skillet. Pour the batter back into the hot skillet and bake until golden brown.

  CRACKLING HOT WATER CORN BREAD

2 cups whole grain cornmeal
2 cups crisp cracklings, broken into small pieces
salt
boiling water
shortening

Put cornmeal into large mixing bowl. Add cracklings and salt. Mix. Add enough boiling water to make stiff dough. Heat a well-greased iron skillet and pour in the batter. Bake in preheated 450° oven until brown.

CHITTERLINGS (CHITLINS)

10 lbs. chitterlings
1 onion
¼ cup vinegar
¼ cup minced garlic
2 stalks celery
1 tablespoon salt
¼ teaspoon black pepper
red pepper, if desired

Batter:
2 eggs
1 cup milk
flour or corn meal

Take approximately 10 pounds of chitterlings (pork intestines) and wash inside and out. (It is very important to clean thoroughly.) Soak overnight in salt water. The next day, remove chitterlings and rinse well.

Drop chitterlings in pot of boiling water and cook about thirty minutes. Add 1 onion, ¼ cup vinegar, ¼ cup minced garlic, 2 stalks celery, 1 tablespoon salt, ¼ teaspoon black pepper, and red pepper (if desired). Cover pot and cook slowly for approximately 3 hours. Remove chitterlings and cut into small pieces. Dip pieces in batter of 2 eggs, 1 cup milk, and enough flour or cornmeal to make thick. (Make more batter when needed.) Fry until golden brown. Salt and pepper to taste.

Tripe may be boiled and fried in the same manner.

FRIED CORN PONES

Fried corn pones can be made using the same ingredients as crackling hot water corn bread. Shape the dough into small oval-shaped pones, and drop them into hot shortening one-eighth inch deep in a skillet. Fry until brown. Drain.

  ### PIGTAILS WITH TURNIP GREENS

Clean pigtail thoroughly, cut into sections, salt and pepper to taste, and brown in shortening. Add 1 cup water, cover and simmer slowly for about 1½ to 2 hours or until tender. Serve with turnip greens.

  ### PICKLED PIGS' FEET

Scald, scrape, and clean twelve pigs' feet. Cover with boiling salted water and simmer for approximately four hours until tender, but not until meat falls off bones. Pack the feet into sterilized jars, cover with boiling special vinegar solution, and seal.

SPECIAL VINEGAR SOLUTION

2 quarts vinegar
2 tablespoons horseradish
1 red pepper, chopped
1 teaspoon whole black pepper
1 bay leaf

Mix all ingredients together, pour into a pan, and bring to a boil.

  FRIED PIGS' FEET

pickled pigs' feet
2 eggs
1 cup milk
salt to season
1 tablespoon melted butter
flour

Split desired amount of pickled pigs' feet and dip each piece in a batter made of 2 eggs, a cup of milk, salt, a tablespoon of melted butter, and enough flour to make thick. Fry in hot grease until crisp.

The Bragg Hotel. (*Courtesy Mrs. Sue Marcontell.*)

B R A G G

THE BRAGG HOTEL

Halloween in the Big Thicket is one of the spookiest times of the year in one of the spookiest places I have ever seen. You may find this hard to believe, but this morning I woke up with the strangest sensation that today something unusual was going to happen. I guess it is just a coincidence that the day I planned to write about the ghostliest hotel in the ghostliest town on the ghostliest road in the ghostly Big Thicket should turn out to be Halloween . . . but then again, maybe it isn't.

Believing that I might capture the flavor of the whole scenario if I were there, I decided to drive out to the Thicket where the old Bragg Hotel once stood and wait for the spirit to move me. All around me the trees dripped with moss and suspense. As I stood there in the gloom, I could hear an owl hooting in the background, and I realized how unusual it was to hear owls in the daytime. I felt my heart beating faster as I slowly ventured up to the site of the old hotel. The closer I got, the more the eerie solitude affected me, and I began to envision all kinds of things. Were they real, or were they just a product of my tormented imagination? Right behind me I heard a train whistle, and I whirled around only to realize there was no train there! Was this an echo from the past, or had I become so carried away that I started hallucinating? At this point, I was just about as tense as I could get,

Inside the
Bragg Hotel.

and I knew that I needed to calm down fast. It was then that I decided
to write down the actual history rather than to stand there creating
my own hysteria.

There is a narrow dirt road that travels eastward for eleven miles as
straight as an arrow to Saratoga. During the boom, the road served
as the Santa Fe tram line for the old Saratoga train which chugged
daily between Bragg and Saratoga transporting people, freight, and
timber.

Even in its heyday, Bragg, named for General Braxton Bragg, a
Civil War soldier and surveyor for the Santa Fe Railroad, never had
more than a handful of people. Small as it was, though, it served two
needed functions of the railroad: a junction for the Saratoga train and
a watering and oiling station for the mainline trains of the Gulf,
Colorado, and Santa Fe Railroad which ran through Bragg between
Beaumont and Somerville.

Henry and Margaret McLean, 1905. *(Courtesy Mrs. Sue Marcontell.)*

The Bragg Hotel was built around 1904 by Mr. Otho Head to take care of the transient people who went to and from the Saratoga oil field, but after his death, the hotel was managed by Mrs. Minnie Cockran until it was sold to Mrs. Margaret McLean in 1910.

Mrs. McLean moved to Bragg in 1907 when her husband Henry went to work there as the depot agent. "She was a beautiful young woman," her daughter Sue Marcontell fondly remembered. And after seeing a wedding picture of her parents, I could see that her mother was lovely indeed.

Mamma and Daddy were married on November 6, 1905, in Gulfport, Mississippi. Right after their wedding, they went to a restaurant to eat, and while sitting at a table, they observed two men tapping on their dinner plates with their fingers. You see, they were telegraph men, and they were sending morse code messages to each other about what a beautiful woman Mamma was. It sure did surprise them when they heard Daddy tapping back another message on his plate. "Thank you very much for the compliment," he said. "The beautiful woman is my wife."

Pretty or not, Mrs. McLean didn't have much time to pamper herself in the semi-wilds of the East Texas piney woods. It was all that she could do to take care of her three small children and complete the many chores involved in running her business. During those early years, the hotel was usually full of people. In addition to the boarders from nearby areas, there were show people from New York and Canada who traveled with the popular road shows. And, like the Kountze Commercial Hotel, the Bragg Hotel sometimes served as the headquarters for the distant bear hunters before they embarked on their forays into the Big Thicket.

Remote living was difficult for the whole family, not just for Mrs. McLean, or her husband who single-handedly manned the depot himself, but for the children as well. Sue's job included milking four cows each morning, walking six miles to school and six miles back no matter what the weather, milking the cows again in the evening, feeding the hogs and chickens, plus helping out with the cooking and cleaning. It made me tired just listening to her, and I could not help but think that there was not any way that I could have endured such a vigorous routine.

If it is true that adversity breeds character, then surely the McLean children must have developed many admirable traits young in life. Particularly, after the unfortunate death of their father from the devastating flu epidemic which swept the nation in 1918, their duties and hardships multiplied. Sue recalled, "Even on Thanksgiving we usually spent the day digging potatoes." However, she confided that at the time, she did not consider her life unusually difficult.

It's funny about those days. People lived in poverty, but nobody thought they did. We always had time to visit with interesting guests and come up with our own games and activities, though.

Santa Fe Depot, Bragg, Texas. (*Courtesy Mrs. Sue Marcontell.*)

Once, we had a crew of Slavonians who came to America to cut staves who stayed with us. The first night they ate with us, we served them turnip greens and they just loved them. The next morning when they came to the table to eat, we had fixed eggs, biscuits, ham, and sausage. But we could tell that they didn't like any of that. They just kept jabberin' away. . . We tried and tried to find out what they wanted, but we couldn't understand them and they couldn't understand us. Finally, one of them got up and went into the kitchen and pointed to the greens. So we fixed it for them. Instead of putting salt and pepper on them, they put syrup. They wanted them three times a day— breakfast, dinner, and supper. They stayed for three weeks and that's all they ate.

We'd always look forward to hog killin' time, because we'd make balloons out of the hogs' bladders. We'd pull weeds which were hollow in the center and use them to blow up the bladders.

In 1921, Mrs. McLean married Walter Ayres, an oil field worker and boarder, but was widowed again several years later. Eventually, the decline in the area's timber and oil activities caused her children and boarders to leave, but she chose to remain in her home until 1979 when, at the age of ninety-three, bad health forced her to leave.

During her long tenure at the hotel, she had weathered economic changes well. Because she was conditioned to make the best of what life had to offer, she was able to accept the discontinuance of the Saratoga train, the removal of the tracks, and the closing of the depot —all factors contributing to Bragg's extinction—as inevitable. However, it was an unexpected twist of fate that actively preserved the identity of Bragg. This particular twist involved the strange appearance of a mysterious light often reportedly seen along the former train line. Rather than enjoying the notoriety generated by ghost stories explaining this extraordinary revelation, she and the other area residents felt it to be more of a burden than a blessing, so it's ironic that it was this very trick of fate that has kept the memory of Bragg alive and well in the hearts of East Texans.

It was soon after the removal of the railroad tracks in the 1930s, when the roadbed became a public road, that tales of the light began to grow. But it wasn't until the 1950s that the local legends began attracting lots of attention from outside the Thicket. On one Halloween night, so many people wanted to see the light for themselves that a constable had to be called to direct the traffic. Some people who claim to have seen the light describe it as being a huge ominous-looking orange ball of fire rampaging through the air, bouncing wildly down the road. Others compare it to a ghostly flashlight with a pin prick of hazy light. Naturally, there are as many different theories about the light as there have been witnesses to it, or the lack thereof, and most of these have managed to find their way into print.

"We hated all the publicity," Sue admitted. "We were constantly being irritated by all the spectators and spirits alike. The creepiest thing that ever happened to us was when our house mysteriously burned on Halloween, right after Mother moved out. And we never found out what caused the fire."

The road was so popular that the Big Thicket Museum in Saratoga began conducting ghost walks in the moonlight. Every year around Halloween, guests were treated to a hayride and were given a two-mile guided tour along the road. While walking down the road, the guides would enhance the mystery of the evening by relating ghost stories and talking about the possibilities of a light appearing. As a volunteer at the museum, I enjoyed helping set the stage for the ghostly trek by telling the fortunes of those hearty souls about to embark on the tour. Being a firm believer that it's better to be safe than sorry, I was happy to keep my vigil from my own little cozy corner of the museum.

Almost every Southeast Texan has either walked down, driven down, or talked about going down Ghost Road on Halloween night. So did I *once*, when we were short-handed at the museum. I took a bunch of teenagers who apparently had more on their minds than ghost stories, but I started my recitation anyway. "You know, some people say that the light is really the lantern carried by a decapitated train engineer who lost his head one night in a train accident. Be careful that nothing happens to you out here tonight that'll make you lose your heads!" I'm not sure they heard my good advice or the rest of my story because they had gotten so far ahead of me that I had to run after them, yelling, "Other people say it shines over the graves of Mexican workmen who were hired to lay the tracks and were murdered by the road foreman who also cheated them out of their wages." By this time, the teenagers had disappeared into the dense woods. "Yoo-hoo, yoo-hoo," I called. "Ya'll need to come out of there. I've heard that there's still plenty of bear and panthers around here!" When there was no answer, I realized that those kids weren't going to come out until they were good and ready. I was either going to have to wait for them in the big middle of nowhere—by myself—or head on back to the truck, which was at least a mile away.

I started back, first walking fast and then running. My heart was pounding fast enough to drown out the sounds I heard all around me. On that Halloween night in the center of the Big Thicket, I was convinced that I'd been chased by a panther, had wrestled a bear, had stepped on at least three snakes, and had dodged an alligator on that short trip back. As I fell into the back of the truck, I heard somebody ask, "Did you see the light?" "No, I didn't," I gasped weakly, "but maybe next year."

I did not see the light everybody's been talking about, but I did see the light of truth—that I wouldn't venture out on Bragg Road ever again, crowd or no crowd.

BRAGG HOTEL RECIPES

Over her more than sixty years as matriarch of the Bragg Hotel, Margaret McLean (Ayres) collected many outstanding recipes which she left as a legacy to her daughter, Sue Marcontell. Sue, in turn, graciously shared a variety of them with me. After applying the taste test, I'll have to agree with a comment I recently heard from a former boarder: "Eating at the Bragg Hotel was like having Sunday dinner everyday."

 ## OLD-FASHIONED MEAT LOAF

1 lb. ground meat
½ lb. ground and seasoned sausage
1 cup bread crumbs
1 cup cracker crumbs
½ cup onion, minced
½ cup bell pepper, finely chopped
½ cup celery, chopped
2 cups tomatoes with juice (canned or fresh)
2 eggs
1 tablespoon salt
1 teaspoon black pepper
1 tablespoon Worcestershire sauce

Mix all ingredients together. Heat 3 tablespoons shortening in baking pan. Pour mixed ingredients in pan and place in oven for approximately 45 minutes at 375° to 400°. Baste often.

COUNTRY STYLE BAKED FISH

Fresh fish, a rare treat at most Big Thicket boarding houses, was frequently served at the Bragg Hotel, especially after the catfish had been biting at nearby Big Sandy Creek and Village Creek. Mrs. McLean did not call her baked fish Sauce Piquant, but her recipe was very similar in taste to the Cajun dish.

4 or 5 lbs. whole fish, heads removed (catfish, bass,
   red fish, or red snapper)

Sauce:
8 tablespoons butter, melted
2 cups onion, finely chopped
2 cups celery, finely chopped
½ cup bell pepper, finely chopped
4 cups tomatoes, chopped (canned tomatoes
   should be drained)
1 tablespoon Worcestershire sauce
juice of ½ lemon
salt and pepper to taste
dash of cayenne pepper

Melt butter in sauce pan. Add onions, celery, and bell pepper. Cook slowly until wilted, being careful not to brown. Add other sauce ingredients. Simmer slowly for approximately 45 minutes, stirring often. Sprinkle fish inside and outside with salt and pepper. Dredge lightly with flour. Place fish in baking dish and cover with sauce. Bake at 350° for approximately 30 to 45 minutes, basting often. Fish should flake easily when tested with a fork.

BAKED DEVILED EGGPLANT CASSEROLE

Complementing the flavor of the baked fish was this eggplant casserole which began to appear on the hotel's bill of fare during the later years.

> 1 large eggplant, peeled and diced
> 2 tablespoons bacon drippings
> 1 medium onion, finely chopped
> ½ cup bell pepper, finely chopped
> 3 tomatoes, peeled and diced
> salt and pepper to taste
> 1 cup grated American cheese
> ¾ cup toasted bread crumbs
> ½ cup butter, melted

Boil eggplant in salted water until tender. Drain. Sauté the onion and bell pepper in bacon drippings. Combine eggplant with onion-bell pepper mixture. Add tomatoes. Salt and pepper to taste. Place mixture in buttered casserole dish to alternate layers with the cheese. Top with bread crumbs and pour melted butter over casserole. Bake for approximately 30 minutes at 350°.

According to Sue Marcontell, her mother was known for her special meat dishes. While many boarding houses did not serve an abundance of beef in the days before refrigeration, Mrs. McLean usually had a supply on hand. "It wasn't pickled," Sue said. "It was canned and sealed. Mother often bought a whole beef at a time and it took two days to process."

CHILI-SPAGHETTI CASSEROLE

3 tablespoons shortening
1 lb. ground beef
½ cup onion, minced
½ cup celery, chopped
1 tablespoon chili powder
1 teaspoon salt
1 12-oz. can tomato paste and an equal amount of water
1 small bottle stuffed olives
1 cup shredded cheddar cheese
1 7-oz. pkg. spaghetti (cook as directed)

Heat shortening in iron skillet. Add ground beef and stir until meat turns white. Add onion, celery, chili powder, and salt. Stir until wilted, being careful not to brown. Add tomato paste and water. Simmer for approximately 45 minutes.

Divide cooked spaghetti. Place one-half in buttered baking dish. Pour one-half chili mixture over spaghetti. Top with sliced olives. Layer again with spaghetti and chili mixture. Top with shredded cheese. Place in oven at 375°. When cheese melts, remove from oven.

FRESH COCONUT CAKE

1 cup butter
2 cups sugar
3 cups flour
2 teaspoons baking powder
pinch of salt
½ cup milk
½ cup water
5 egg whites, beaten until frothy
½ teaspoon vanilla

Cream the butter and sugar and then beat until light and fluffy.
Combine the flour, baking powder, and salt. Add the flour mixture
to the creamed mixture alternately with the milk and water. Fold in
egg whites and stir in the vanilla. Pour into four well-greased and
floured cake pans. Bake at 375° for 20 to 25 minutes. Cool completely.
Ice with coconut frosting.

 COCONUT FROSTING

2 cups light corn syrup
3 egg whites, beaten until frothy
pinch of salt
1 teaspoon vanilla
2 to 3 cups fresh coconut, grated

Pour corn syrup into top of double boiler and heat until boiling. Pour
in beaten egg whites, beating constantly. Add the salt and vanilla and
continue beating until stiff peaks form. Frost between layers and top
and side of cake with mixture, sprinkling generously with fresh coconut.

SWEET POTATO PIE DELUXE

2 cups cooked sweet potatoes, firmly packed
⅔ cup sugar
3 egg yolks
½ teaspoon salt
1 teaspoon cinnamon
½ teaspoon nutmeg
½ teaspoon ginger
¼ teaspoon cloves
1 can canned milk
1 tablespoon flour
¼ cup butter
meringue
1 9-inch unbaked pie crust

Mix all ingredients and pour into unbaked pie shell. (See East Texas Hotel recipes, page 118, for pie crust recipe.) Bake at 350° for approximately 40 minutes. Top with meringue and continue baking at 475° until meringue browns.

 ## MERINGUE

3 egg whites
⅛ teaspoon cream of tartar
⅛ teaspoon baking powder
½ cup sugar
¼ teaspoon nutmeg

Beat egg whites (room temperature) until they begin to foam. Add cream of tartar and baking powder and continue beating. Just before mixture becomes fully stiff, add sugar gradually along with nutmeg.

FRANKLIN NUT CAKE

1 lb. butter
2 cups sugar
6 eggs
4 cups flour
1 teaspoon baking powder
¼ teaspoon salt
½ lb. candied cherries
½ lb. candied pineapple
1 lb. pecans
2 teaspoons vanilla

Cream the butter and sugar well. Add the eggs, one at a time, beating well after each. Sift 3 cups of the flour and the baking powder together. Add to the creamed mixture. Coat the cherries, pineapple, and broken nuts with the remaining flour. Stir into the batter. Add vanilla. Pour into a tube cake pan that has been greased and floured well. Bake at 250° for approximately 2 hours. Cool before removing from pan.

 MOLASSES SUGAR CRISPS

1½ cups butter
2 cups sugar
½ cup molasses
2 eggs
4 teaspoons soda
4 cups sifted flour
1 teaspoon cloves
1 teaspoon ginger
2 teaspoons cinnamon
1 teaspoon salt
sugar for coating

Cream butter and sugar well. Add molasses and eggs, beating well. Sift together remaining dry ingredients. Add to first mixture. Mix well and chill thoroughly. Form in 1-inch balls. Roll in sugar. Place on greased cookie sheets 2 inches apart. Bake at 375° for 8 to 10 minutes.

CUSTARD FRUIT CUPS

Fast foods were unheard of during the boarding house era, but this tasty quick-cooking custard dish was often served on the busiest of days.

    peach halves
    1 cup grated coconut

Custard Sauce:
    2 cups milk
    4 egg yolks, slightly beaten
    ½ cup sugar
    ⅓ cup cornstarch
    1 teaspoon vanilla

Cook first 4 custard sauce ingredients in top of double boiler over medium heat until mixture thickens, stirring constantly. Remove from heat, stir in vanilla, and cool.

Line small bowl with peach halves (one on bottom and two along sides of dish). Spoon an ample amount of custard into the dish and sprinkle with grated coconut.

BREAD AND RICE PUDDING

1 cup cooked rice
1 cup toasted bread crumbs
½ cup sugar
2 cups milk
2 eggs, slightly beaten
½ teaspoon nutmeg
½ cup seedless raisins, softened with hot water
¼ teaspoon salt

Mix all ingredients together. Pour into greased baking pan and bake at 350° for approximately 1 hour or until firm.

If desired, serve with lemon or raisin cream sauce. (See Cariker Hotel recipes for lemon sauce, page 93.) (See East Texas Hotel recipes, page 120, for raisin cream sauce.)

EPILOGUE

While researching and writing this book, I often found myself wondering what it would be like to step back in time for perhaps a day or two, board a slow-moving train, and stop for visits at some of the early Thicket hotels and boarding houses . . . . Who knows? Maybe, if I concentrate enough, I can . . .

"All aboard! All aboard!" It is the conductor of the Santa Fe "Doodlebug" calling. I had better hurry because the train is about to pull out! But even if it does leave, I can probably catch it. . . . My goodness! Is the train coming off its track? This car is moving so much that I can hardly sit in my seat. And it's hot in here! . . .

"Conductor, is there something wrong with the air conditioning?" . . . Why is everyone looking at me so strangely? Oh, I forgot—they don't know about refrigerated air. . . . Well, it won't be long until we arrive in Silsbee; I will try to relax and enjoy the scenery. Just looking out of the window at the magnificent trees and smelling their fresh aroma makes me feel better. It is too bad that the forest is being cut-over by the timber companies. I know there is a need for trees, but what is going to happen when they are gone?

The Kirby Mill whistle is blowing, so we are nearing Silsbee. After this unsteady ride, it'll feel good to get off the train, stretch a bit, and have lunch. I will eat at the Badders Hotel because the food is always good there. . . . Who is that woman being chased out the front door by Mrs. Badders? It must be another one of those crooked women. . . .

And there is May Badders throwing lethal objects at her brothers. Things are much too lively there; I'll walk over to the Harvey House instead. Their food is delicious, also, even if they do cut the meat so thin. It'll be a pleasure visiting with the friendly Harvey House girls who look attractive in their crisp uniforms.

Someone told me that the drummers are exhibiting Christmas merchandise at the Commercial Hotel in Kountze. I'll board the train again and stop there for awhile. Only merchants are allowed in the showroom, but since I am related to the Bradleys, maybe they'll let me look at the beautiful clothes. Come to think of it, they do not realize I exist. Perhaps I shouldn't get off the train at all . . . . From the distance, I can hear Grandpa Bradley calling, "Commercial Hotel! Commercial Hotel!" He surely is a mercenary soul, trying his best to corner the market on the hotel business in the town. Because he does not know that I am his great-granddaughter, I'll just wave and not speak. Besides, he looks grumpy . . . Look, here comes John Foster, limping down the road! He and Mrs. Cariker must be getting along well today because he is greeting everyone he passes and singing "Honey Island." . . . I know one thing, I am not spending the night in Honey Island! Some of the people in the hotel there get too noisy, especially at night. . . Things are much calmer at the Bragg Hotel. The most excitement they have is serving mustard greens to the "Slavonians." I will get off there, catch the Saratoga train, and spend the night at the Vines with "Aunt Matt" Evans and her nephew, Lance Rosier. . . The passengers on this train do not seem to be nervous about the ghost light. Just wait until the tracks come up; then they will see it!

I cannot decide who is standing on Aunt Matt's porch because the vines are so thick that they are obstructing my view. . . It is Lance! He is putting a cold sweet potato and some bacon into a brown paper sack. He must be going out into the Thicket again to identify more plants. People say that he'd rather tramp through the woods than take part in one of Aunt Matt's hog killings. Who could blame him for that! Besides, one day he may be famous.

If the water is down in Pine Island Bayou tomorrow, I will hire someone to drive me in a wagon to Aunt Doll's boarding house in

Batson. The trip will be long and uncomfortable over the corduroy road, but it will be worth it because Aunt Doll is having a get-together to celebrate her marriage to "Fete" Caruthers.

The ride was not fun, but I am still in the mood for a party. I can hear the Caruthers family tuning their fiddles and guitars for a good old country hoedown . . . I had better hurry! . . . What was that I stepped in? A smoking cow chip! Well, at least it is hard and crusty . . . "Hi, everyone . . . No, thank you, I'll pass on the tripe."

Fantasies about earlier days may be amusing pastimes, but I do not think anyone would actually want to trade his life for that of his ancestors. The older ways may have been slower-paced and less stressful, but the monotony of providing for basic needs consumed almost everyone's waking hours. Modern conveniences and faster modes of travel indeed have allowed us more leisure time to expand our horizons. Who is to say which way is better? But when it comes to food, I will take the old-timey cooking any day!

So rather than dream about the past, I think I will drive to Woodville and have lunch at the Pickett House. The building is not authentic; it was once an old schoolhouse, but the boarding house atmosphere and the flavor of the food are just about as real as you can get.

The early Big Thicket hotels and boarding houses are gone now; but I hope that these reminiscences and recipes will last forever.

BIBLIOGRAPHY

A. PRIMARY SOURCES

1. CORRESPONDENCE TO AUTHOR

Barineau, Bessie. 24 October 1988.
Caton, Carter. January 1979.
Day, Joyce. 2 October 1979.
Hooper, Mildred. 17 September 1985.
Leggett, Vera. May 1979.

2. INTERVIEWS WITH AUTHOR

Abshire, Pat. Daisetta, Texas, 13 April 1984.
Adams, Judy. Beaumont, Texas, 4 June 1985.
Addington, Floyd. Jasper, Texas, 7 February 1985.
Alexander, Doris. Beaumont, Texas, November 1980.
Barnes, B. B. Chester, Texas, January 1985.
Barnes, Mary Lou. Chester, Texas, January 1985.
Bledsoe, Carl T. Jasper, Texas, 20 March 1985.
Boyd, Eda Belle. Daisetta, Texas, 15 March 1984.
Boyt, Sue. Devers, Texas, 23 October 1984.
Brandt, Jo. Austin, Texas, 28 October 1985.
Brett, Bill. Hull, Texas, 20 October 1985.

Bruce, Kate. Sour Lake, Texas, 16 October 1979.
Busby, Emma. Woodville, Texas, 15 April 1985.
Bush, L. W. Huntsville, Texas, 27 March 1985.
Callahan, Hortense. Houston, Texas, 12 February 1985.
Cariker, Miley Mayo. Kountze, Texas, 27 July 1978.
Cariker, W. B. Kountze, Texas, 27 July 1978.
Carpenter, Harold. Sour Lake, Texas, November 1979.
Childers, Bess M. Jasper, Texas, June 1978.
Coley, Harriette Bonner. Saratoga, Texas, 25 April 1985.
Combs, Joe. Beaumont, Texas, 13 October 1977.
Crain, Don. Beaumont, Texas, 17 August 1978.
Crain, Kay. Beaumont, Texas, 17 August 19778.
Crews, Alvin. Colmesneil, Texas, September 1978.
Crews, Minnie. Beaumont, Texas, 9 February 1984.
Crews, Ruth. Colmesneil, Texas, September 1978.
Crosby, Hettie. Kountze, Texas, 9 May 1985.
Duncan, Fay. Port Arthur, Texas, 11 June 1985.
Durham, Aaron. Colmesneil, Texas, 25 January 1985.
Echols, Mrs. Jack. Liberty, Texas, October 1984.
Enloe, Betty. Colmesneil, Texas, September 1978.
Erickson, L. T. Beaumont, Texas, 21 January 1985.
Fain, J. Wood. Woodville, Texas, 8 February 1985.
Foster, Alfrieda. Houston, Texas, 12 February 1981.
_____. Houston, Texas, 12 February 1985.
Fregia, Marie. Daisetta, Texas, 9 February 1985.
Greenwood, Fay Dell. West Columbia, Texas, 14 March 1985.
Hancock, Fay S. Jasper, Texas, 20 February 1985.
Hancock, Sarah Ann Bledsoe. Jasper, Texas, 20 March 1985.
Hardage, Anna Mae. Sour Lake, Texas, 16 October 1979.
Hargrove, Alma. Silsbee, Texas, 23 January 1984.
Hargrove, Kate. Silsbee, Texas, 23 January 1984.
Hart, J. M. Batson, Texas, 9 April 1985.
Hendrix, C. W. Honey Island, Texas, 9 May 1985.
Hendrix, Henry C. Doucette, Texas, 19 May 1985.
Herndon, Lexie. Kirbyville, Texas, February 1983.
Herrington, Ruby. Kountze, Texas, November 1977.

Hines, Earl S. Burkeville, Texas, 7 February 1985.
Hines, Pauline. Burkeville, Texas, 7 February 1985.
Hobbs, Clyde E. Batson, Texas, 27 April 1985.
Holland, Irene. Silsbee, Texas, 14 December 1983.
Holland, W. H. Silsbee, Texas, 14 December 1983.
Holmes, W. L. Honey Island, Texas, 9 May 1985.
Hooks, Geraldine. Kountze, Texas, 16 May 1985.
Hooks, Thomas Sidney. Kountze, Texas, 16 October 1985.
Houlihan, James. Jasper, Texas, 12 March 1985.
Ingram, Lola. Jasper, Texas, 12 March 1985.
Jackson, Helen. Jasper, Texas, 7 February 1985.
Johnson, Mrs. Ed. Grayburg, Texas, November 1979.
Johnson, Eda. Batson, Texas, 8 February 1983.
Johnson, Nelda. Kountze, Texas, 16 April 1985.
Johnson, Versie L. Kountze, Texas, 13 May 1985.
Kaine, Nell. Buna, Texas, 18 April 1985.
King, Walton "Smooth". Sour Lake, Texas, November 1979.
Lee, Virginia. Houston, Texas, 13 March 1985.
Lewis, Irene. Chester, Texas, March 1979.
Loftin, Mamie Bell. Saratoga, Texas, 9 April 1985.
Lucas, Doris Hayes. Trinity, Texas, November 1980.
Lucius, Letitia. Beaumont, Texas, 8 June 1978.
McBride, Mayo. Woodville, Texas, 15 April 1985.
McCreight, Ethel E. Batson, Texas, 1 May 1985.
McCreight, Walter L. Batson, Texas, 15 March 1985.
McKim, Minnie O. Kountze, Texas, 17 January 1985.
Mann, Bob. Lufkin, Texas, 4 February 1985.
Mann, Easter. Colmesneil, Texas, 31 October 1978.
Marcontell, Susie McLean. Port Arthur, Texas, April 1980.
Marshall, Nida. Jasper, Texas, 12 March 1985.
Martin, Juanita. Saratoga, Texas, 3 April 1985.
Matthews, Dallas. Jasper, Texas, 7 February 1985.
Mattox, Beatrice. Houston, Texas, 6 March 1985.
Middleton, B. Jasper, Texas, 20 February 1985.
Mobley, Ollie Mae. Jasper, Texas, 14 February 1985.
Moore, Archie. Honey Island, Texas, 9 May 1985.

Moseley, Lou Ella. Colmesneil, Texas, 31 October 1978.
Mowbray, Jessie Lea. Sour Lake, Texas, August 1988.
Nerren, Joe Byrd. Moscow, Texas, 25 January 1985.
Neushafer, James. Beaumont, Texas, June 1980.
Newbold. W. H. Buna, Texas, 6 February 1984.
Nickells, W. M. Saratoga, Texas, April 1985.
Nixson, Eugenia. Silsbee, Texas, January 1981.
—————————. Buna, Texas, 9 February 1985.
Norrid, A. S. Beaumont, Texas, 18 January 1985.
Overland, Erie May. Silsbee, Texas, 7 February 1984.
Parker, Albert. Kountze, Texas, 16 May 1985.
Powell, Faye. Kirbyville, Texas, 21 March 1985.
Powell, Frank. Kirbyville, Texas, 21 March 1985.
Rae, Massie. Newton, Texas, October 1978.
Ralph, Ira D. Jasper, Texas, 20 March 1985.
Rainey, H. L. Woodville, Texas, November 1979.
Reichelt, Ed. Bessmay, Texas, November 1984.
—————————. Kirbyville, Texas, 21 March 1985.
Richardson, Mary F. Kountze, Texas, 17 January 1985.
Richey, Bennie. Beaumont, Texas, 29 April 1985.
Rischard, Ferrelle. Kirbyville, Texas, 10 February 1981.
Riviere, Virgie. Liberty, Texas, October 1983.
Rosier, James Elmo. Votaw, Texas, 19 March 1984.
Ryan, Allie. Saratoga, Texas, 25 April 1985.
St. Ores, Viola. Lumberton, Texas, November 1984.
Sanders, Ila. Kountze, Texas, 9 November 1977.
Scurlock, Carrie Conn. Buna, Texas, 18 April 1985.
Scurlock, Robert. Buna, Texas, 18 April 1985.
Seamans, C. A. Chester, Texas, March 1979.
Seamans, Zelda. Chester, Texas, March 1979.
Sells, Mary. Kountze, Texas, 13 May 1985.
Skinner, Beulah. Saratoga, Texas, 3 April 1985.
Skinner, W. E. Bessmay, Texas, November 1984.
Smith, Calvin. Wiergate, Texas, 22 January 1985.
Smith, Pickney. Daisetta, Texas, 20 October 1985.
Sory, Mrs. Lewis. Livingston, Texas, 8 March 1979.

Stalsby, E. Saratoga, Texas, 3 April 1985.
Sutton, Ruby. Port Neches, Texas, November 1980.
Thomas, Robert Otis. Somerville, Texas, 14 June 1985.
Thornton, Inez. Chester, Texas, March 1979.
Tompkins, Cadillac. Daisetta, Texas, 20 October 1985.
Van Deventer, Nita. Beaumont, Texas, 16 November 1984.
Watson, Jesse R. Beaumont, Texas, October 1979.
Watts, Mrs. Jack. Moscow, Texas, 25 January 1985.
Wells, Bessie. Saratoga, Texas, 15 March 1985.
West, Minnie. Batson, Texas, 27 April 1985.
Williams, Margaret Skinner. Saratoga, Texas, 3 April 1985.
Williamson, Ben. Jasper, Texas, 4 June 1985.
Williford, Aline. Kountze, Texas, 11 April 1985.
Williford, T. C. Kountze, Texas, 11 April 1985.
Wright, Ada P. King. Grayburg, Texas, November 1979.
Wright, Lon. Beaumont, Texas, October 1978.
Wynne, G. W. Kirbyville, Texas, 29 March 1985.

3. NEWSPAPERS

Galveston Daily News, 14 July 1857.
Galveston Daily News, 28 August 1883.
Houston Tri-weekly Telegram, 21 October 1865.

B. SECONDARY SOURCES

1. BOOKS

Abernethy, Francis E. *Tales from the Big Thicket.* Austin: University of
   Texas Press, 1966.
Landrey, Wanda A. *Outlaws in the Big Thicket.* Austin: Eakin Publica-
   tions, 1976.

Moseley, Lou Ella. *Pioneer Days of Tyler County.* Woodville, Texas: Tyler County Heritage Society, Inc., 1985.

Pictorial History of Polk County Texas (1846-1910). The Heritage Committee of the Polk County Bicentennial Committee and the Polk County Historical Commission, Revised edition, 1978.

2. NEWSPAPERS

Beaumont Enterprise. 30 June 1940.
_____. 11 January 1970.
_____. 4 February 1973.
_____. 6 May 1973.
_____. 2 June 1974.
_____. 24 November 1978.
_____. 28 February 1983.
East Texas News. 21 July 1982.
Houston Chronicle. 4 August 1968.
Kountze News. 15 January 1970.
Pine Needle. 19 January 1967.

3. PERIODICALS

Cox, James A. "How Good Food and Harvey 'Skirts' Won the West," *Smithsonian* (September 1987): 130-140.

Crumbaker, Marge. "Saratoga's Mysterious Ghost Light," *Tempo Magazine (The Houston Post)* 3, no. 50 (December 13, 1970): 6-10.

4. UNPUBLISHED ARTICLES AND MANUSCRIPTS

Block, W. T. "Emerald of the Neches: The Chronicles of Beaumont, Texas from Reconstruction to Spindletop," 1980, Nederland, Texas.

"Fred Harvey and the American West," A Teacher/Discussion Leader's Guide, from the files of Jean Irwin, Railroad Museum, Galveston, Texas.

Merrem, W. E. "Thirty-seven Years with the Houston Oil Company of Texas, Southwestern Settlement and Development Company and East Texas Pulp and Paper Company," January, 1975, Houston, Texas.

"Sour Lake, Texas: Health Resort of the Nineteenth Century," from the personal files of Lois Williams Parker, Beaumont, Texas.

INDEX

A
Alabama, 142
Amfac, 50
Ammans family, 124-126
Andrews, Jim, 110
Appetizers:
A Zesty Appetizer, 53
Creamed Stuffed Eggs, 55
Arline, Carrie, 92
Atchison, Topeka, and Santa Fe
Railroad, 47
Aunt Doll, 127-130, 176
Aunt Doll's Boarding House, 123-
137, 129, 175
Aunt Hettie, 5
Aunt Matt (see Evans, Mattie), 141-
144, 141, 142, 143, 147, 175
Aunt Phein, 88-89, 91
Aunt Phein's Bread Pudding, 93
Ayres, Walter, 161

B
Badders family, 31-36
Badders Hotel, 28, 29-45, 174
Badders, Mary Elizabeth Clark, 31,
33, 33-35, 40, 174
Badders, William James, 31
Baked Deviled Eggplant Casserole,
166

Baked Sweet Potatoes, 136
Baking Powder Biscuits, 84
Bannister, Totsy, 114
Barnes, Jesse Bill, 86
Batson, 122, 123-130, 125, 176
Beans:
Mrs. Nixson's Chili Beans, 43
Bear Meat, 27
Beaumont, xv, xvi, xviii, xix, 3,
38, 109, 110, 111, 112, 158
Beaumont Enterprise, 110
Beef Rissoles with Mashed Potatoes,
58
Beef Tea, 11
Beeson, Gwen, xvi
Berry Cobbler, 137
Bessmay, 63-67
Bessmay Cemetery Homecoming,
63
Bessmay Hotel, 63-71, 65
Big Sandy Creek, 165
Big Thicket Museum, 14, 138, 140,
143, 145, 162
Big Thicket National Preserve, 146
Biscuits:
Baking Powder Biscuits, 84
Cheese Biscuits, 55
Black Cat Jim, 124
Boyd, Eda Belle, 15-16

Bracken family, xii
Bradley family, 1-5, 175
Bradley, Barney, 1
Bradley, Ila, *xxiv*, 1, 3, *3*
Bradley, Jim (Grandpa), xix, 1, 4-5
Bradley, Melissa (Grandma), *xxiv*, 1, 6, 11
Bradley, Mittye, *xxiv*, 1, 5
Bragg, 157-163, *161*
Bragg, Braxton, 158
Bragg Hotel, *156*, 157-173, *158*, 175
Bragg Road, 163
Brains and Eggs, 150
Brakin, Ola, *3*
Bray, Mable, xvi, 63
Brazile (see Dr. Mud), 18-20
Bread and Rice Pudding, 173
Bread:
   Crackling Corn Bread, 152
   Crackling Hot Water Corn
     Bread, 152
Brown Gravy, 59
*Bull Cook and Authentic Historical
   Recipes*, 10
Burwick, Minnie, ix, 87-88
Butter Cake, 45

C
C. B., 128
Cake:
   Butter Cake, 45
   Devil's Food Cake, 104
   Franklin Nut Cake, 170
   Fresh Coconut Cake, 168
   Jam Cake, 8-9
   Jelly Cake, 70
   Mrs. Badders Steamed Fruitcake,
     40-41
   One-Two-Three-Four Cake, 131

Caledonia, 123-137
Canada, 160
Caplen, George, xiv
Cariker, Cecile, 86
Cariker family, 87-90
Cariker Hotel, 86, 87-93
Cariker, Nora, 86, 87-89, 175
Cariker, Mrs. W. B., 86, 92
Cariker, W. P., 87
Caruthers, Lafayette "Fete", 127-130, 176
Cheese Biscuits, 55
Cheese Soufflé, 57
Chester, xv
Chicago, 2
Chicken and Dressing, 114
Chicken and Dumplings, 91
Chicken Pot Pie, 6
Chicken Ranch, 99
Childress, Dorothy, 94
Chili-Spaghetti Casserole, 167
Chitterlings, 153
Chocolate Pie, 71
Christmas, 32, 40, 66, 175
Circa 100, 110, *111*
City Hotel, 29-39, *35*, *36*, *37*
Clam Chowder, 54
Cleveland, Grover, 18
Cobbler:
   Berry Cobbler, 137
Cockran, Minnie, 159
Coconut Cake, 168
Coconut Frosting, 168
Collins family, xii
Collins, Lizzie, 64, 68, 70
Collins, V. A. xiii,
Collins, Warren, xiii
Colmesneil, 109-112
Colmesneil, W. T., 109

Comeaux, Lynda, 40
Commercial Hotel, xxi, *xxiv*, 3, 1-
    11, 87, 160, 175
Cookies:
    Ginger Cookies, 42
    Molasses Sugar Crisps, 171
    Oatmeal Cookies, 103
    Old-Fashioned Tea Cakes, 132
Corned Beef Hash, 56
Corned Beef Hash and Eggs, 57
Cotton, Alice, *15*
Country Style Baked Fish, 165
Country-Style Hominy, 116
Crackling Corn Bread, 152
Crackling Hot Water Corn Bread,
    152
Cracklings, 151
Crain, Don, 110
Cream Gravy, 81
Creamed Stewed Onions, 135
Creamed Stuffed Eggs, 55
Crews, Cora, *xxiv*
Crews, Frank, *xx*
Crews, Lester, 88
Crews, Minnie, ix
Crews, Wanda, *xxiii*
Crews' Meat Market and Package
    Store, xix
Custard Fruit Cups, 172

D
Daisetta, 15
Dallas, 48
Death Valley, 51
Dennis, Dora, 96-97
Desserts (see also Cake, Ice Cream,
    Pie, etc.):
    Aunt Phein's Bread Pudding, 93

Berry Cobbler, 137
Bread and Rice Pudding, 173
Butter Cake, 45
Chocolate Pie, 71
Custard Fruit Cups, 172
Devil's Food Cake, 104
Egg Custard Pie, 9
Franklin Nut Cake, 170
Fresh Coconut Cake, 168
Gingerbread with Raisin Sauce,
    120
Indian Pudding, 119
Jam Cake, 8-9
Jelly Cake, 70
Lemon Chess Pie, 106
Mrs. Badders Steamed Fruitcake,
    40-41
Old-Fashioned Fudge, 107
Pecan Torte, 61
One-Two-Three-Four Cake, 131
Southern Pecan Pie, 118
Sweet Potato Pie Deluxe, 169
Vanilla Custard Ice Cream, 69
Vinegar Pie, 83
Devil's Food Cake, 104
Douglas, William O., 146
Dr. Mud, 18-20
Dr. Paul, 17-18
Dr. Richardson, 21
Dried Venison, 22
Dumplings, 91
Durham, Aaron, 113

E
East Texas Hotel, *108*, 109-121
Edmondson, Ray, *15,17*
Egg Custard Pie, 9
El Tovar Hotel, 51

Evans, Bobby, *143*, 143-144
Evans, Mattie "Aunt Matt", 141-144, *141*, *142*, *143*, 147, 175
Extracta (see Beef Tea), 11

F
Fannin Street, 124
Ferguson, 111, 112
Fish:
    Clam Chowder, 54
    Country Style Baked Fish, 165
Flora Hotel, 87
Ford, Tennessee Ernie, 64
Foster, Alfreida, *72*, 74, *75*, 75-78, 77, 79, 83
Foster, John, 88-90, 95, 175
Fowl:
    Chicken and Dressing, 114
    Chicken and Dumplings, 91
    Chicken Pot Pie, 6
    Fried Chicken, 133
Franklin Nut Cake, 170
Fred Harvey Company, 48, 49, 52
French-Fried Onions, 45
Fresh Coconut Cake, 168
Fresh Shelled Peas, 69
Fried Chicken, 133
Fried Corn Pones, 154
Fried Frog Legs, 134
Fried Hominy, 116
Fried Pigs' Feet, 155
Fried Salt Pork, 151
Fullingim, Archer, xiii

G
Galveston, 2, 16-17, 36, 46, 50, 52
Galveston Daily News, 16, 21
Galveston Historical Society, 52

Galvez Hotel, 37
Ghost Road, 163
Giblet Gravy, 115
Ginger Cookies, 42
Gingerbread with Raisin Cream Sauce, 120
Grand Canyon, 51
Gravy:
    Brown Gravy, 59
    Cream Gravy, 81
    Giblet Gravy, 115
    Red-Eye Gravy, 10
Green, Hortense, 74, 76-77, 82, 85
Gulf, Colorado, and Santa Fe Railroad, 46, 50, 52, 158
Gulfport, Mississippi, 159

H
Halley's Comet, 3
Halloween, 64, 157, 162-163
Hansford, Edna, xvi
Hardage, Anna Mae, *15*
Hardin County, xiv, xviii, 2
Hardin County Fair, 38
Hardy, Thelma, xvi
Hart, Jude, 127
Harvey, Fred, 50-51
Harvey Houses, 35, 46, 47-61, *48*, *49*
Hawkins family, 124
Haynes Settlement, 89
Head, Otho, 159
Hendrix, C. W., xv, xvi
Herrington, Ruby, 3, 11
Herter, Bertha E., 10
High Island, 13
Hill family, 111-112
Hill, Joe, 111

Hobbs, Buck, 128
Hog Killin' Day, 147-148
Hog's Head Cheese, 150
Holland, Homer, 63, 68, 70
Holland, Irene, 68, 70
Holmes, Lester, 95, 97
Homemade Sausage, 115
Honey Island, xvi, 90, 95-100, 175
Honey Island Boarding House, 94,
   95-107
Honeymoon Hotel, 128
Hook family, xii
Hooks' Camp, 2
Houston, 2, 48
Houston, Sam, 19
Husband, Dee, *51*

I
Ice Cream:
   Vanilla Custard Ice Cream, 69
Icing and Frosting:
   Coconut Frosting, 168
   Icing for Jam Cake, 9
   Icing for Pecan Torte, 61
   Seven-Minute Frosting, 105
Indian Pudding, 119

J
Jackson, Andrew, 10
Jackson, Stephen, 14-15
Jam Cake, 8-9
Jasper, xv
Jellies and Preserves:
   Pear Preserves, 82
Jelly Cake, 70
Johnson, 99-100
Johnson, Eda Ammans, *122*, 124,
   125, 130

Johnson, Versie, 88
Johnston, Albert Sidney, 36
Jordan, Thomas C., 142-143

K
Kansas City, Missouri, 52
Kentucky, 110
Kirby Commissary, 64
Kirby, Jim, 30
Kirby, John Henry, 29, 31, 35, 40,
   62, 62, 63, 64-66
Kirby Mill, 174
Kirby Mill Hotel, 29
Kountze, xii, xv, xix, 1-5, 31, 87-90,
   175
Kountze News, The, xiii

L
La Grange, 99
Larache, Lavinia Davis, 126-127
Lemon Chess Pie, 106
Lemon Sauce, 93
Leonard, George, 10
Lewis, Thomasee, xvi
Liberty, xv
Liberty County, xviii
'Lil Angel, 99-100
Liver and Lights (Lungs), 151
Long family, 36
Long, Huey P., 36-37
Lucas, Elizabeth, 31
Lye Soap, 85

M
Magnolia Refinery, xv
Mann family, 111-112
Mann, Dave, 112

Mann, Easter Matthews, 109, 112, 113, 114
Marcontell, Sue, *156, 159*, 159, *161*, 164, 166
Marriott, Joe, 65-66
Marshall, Nida, xv
Mashed Potatoes, 58
Matthews family, 110, 112
Matthews, Savilla, 113
Maybelle, 98-100
Mayonnaise, 60
McBride, Mayo, 111
McCreight, Ethel Richey, 128, *129*, 133, 134
McCreight, Walter, 127-128
McKim, Minnie, 3
McLean, Henry, *159*, 159-160
McLean, Margaret, *159*, 159-161, 164, 165, 166
McMath, Lela, 66-67
McMath, Virginia Katherine, 66-67
Mearns, Betty, xv
Meat and Main Dishes:
  Chili-Spaghetti Casserole, 167
  Corned Beef Hash, 56
  Corned Beef Hash and Eggs, 57
  Cracklings, 151
  Dried Venison, 22
  Fried Frog Legs, 134
  Fried Pigs' Feet, 155
  Fried Salt Pork, 151
  Hog's Head Cheese, 150
  Homemade Sausage, 115
  Liver and Lights (Lungs), 151
  Meat Loaf, 102
  Old-Fashioned Meat Loaf, 164
  Pan-Fried Steak, 80
  Pan-Fried Venison, 22

Pickled Pigs' Feet, 154
Pigtails with Turnip Greens, 154
Preserving Pork, 149
Roast Duck, 26
Roast Goose, 26
Roast Squirrel, 26
Spicy Roast, 92
Squirrel and Dumplings, 25
Squirrel Stew, 24
Stew, 68
Venison Chili, 23
Venison Roast, 23
Meat Loaf, 102
Medicinal:
  Beef Tea, 11
  Sassafras Tea, 121
Meringue, 71, 169
Miss Kitty, 76
Miz Babin, 100
Mobil, xv
Mobile, 2
Molasses Sugar Crisps, 171
Montgomery, John M., 19
Moscow, 74
Moseley, Lou Ella, 110
Mowbray, Jessie Lea, 22
Mowbray, Preston, 22
Mr. Big Thicket (see Rosier, Lance), xi, 142, 144-146, *145*, 175
Mr. Will, 88-89
Mrs. Badders Steamed Fruitcake, 40-41
Mrs. Nixson's Chili Beans, 43

N
Naney, Lee, *142*
New Orleans, 2, 18
New York, 160

Nixson, Eugenia, 30-31, *30, 36, 37,* 39, 43, 44, 45
Nome, 16
Norrid, A. S., 31, 35, 36-38, 43
Norrid, Albert Sidney, 36-37
Norrid, Mary Elizabeth, *34,* 36-39
Norton family, 5

O
Oatmeal Cookies, 103
Ogden, 109
Okra and Tomatoes, 81
Old Hickory, 10
Old-Fashioned Fudge, 107
Old-Fashioned Meat Loaf, 164
Old-Fashioned Tea Cakes, 132
One-Two-Three-Four Cake, 131
Outlaws in the Big Thicket, 4
Overland, May, *28,* 31-35, *33,* 40, 175
Overland, William, 34
Overstreet family, xii

P
Palace, 110, *111,* 112
Pan-Fried Steak, 80
Pan-Fried Venison, 22
Parker family, 94, 101
Parker, Lois, 89, 100
Payne, David, xv, *20*
Pear Preserves, 82
Pecan Torte, 61
Pepper Relish, 101
Petrified Forest Painted Desert, 51
Phillips, May, 66
Pickett House, 176
Pickled Pigs' Feet, 154
Pies:

Chocolate Pie, 71
Egg Custard Pie, 9
Lemon Chess Pie, 106
Southern Pecan Pie, 118
Sweet Potatoe Pie Deluxe, 169
Vinegar Pie, 83
Pigtails with Turnip Greens, 154
Pine Island Bayou, 175
Polk County, xviii
Port Neches, xvi
Preserving Pork, 149
Price, Nancy, 65

R
Raisin Cream Sauce, 120
Read, James, xv
Red-Eye Gravy, 10
Reddings family, 1
Reichelt, Ed, 64, 65
Relish:
    Pepper Relish, 101
Richey, Ethel, *129*
Rio Bravo Boarding House, 5
Roast Duck, 26
Roast Goose, 26
Roast Squirrel, 26
Robertson, Andrew, 98
Rodgers, Jimmie, 129
Rogers, Ginger, 67
Rolls:
    Yeast Rolls, 44
Rosier, Elmo, *141, 142,* 142-146
Rosier, Lance, xi, 142, 144-146, *145*
175
Rushing, Leah, xvi

S
Salads:

Tomato-Cheese Salad, 53
Santa Fe Doodlebug, xix, 174
Santa Fe Railroad, 2, 30, 35, 48, 50, 158
Sapp, Emory Eran, 4
Sapp, Louis, 4
Saratoga, xvi, 2, 5, 123, 124, 139-146, 158-159, 162, 175
Sassafras Tea, 121
Sauces:
  Custard Sauce, 172
  Lemon Sauce, 93
  Mayonnaise, 60
  Raisin Cream Sauce, 120
  Sauce for Baked Fish, 165
  White Sauce, 55
Sauerkraut, 117
Schnick, LaDonna Crews, xx
Scott Hotel, 73-85
Scott, Mattie, *72*, 73, 75-78, *79*
Scott, Walter, 73-78, *75*
Seven-Minute Frosting, 105
Shreveport Times, 36
Silsbee, *29-39*, 48, 50, *51*, 174
Silsbee, Nathaniel, 29
Sims Hotel, 87
Skinner, Bill, 64
Slavonians, 161, 175
Somerville, *49*, 50, 158
Soup:
  Clam Chowder, 54
Sour Lake, xv, 13-20, *20*, 123
Southeast Texas, 2, 47-51
Southern Pecan Pie, 118
Spanish Rice, 102
Special Vinegar Solution, 155
Spicy Roast, 92
Springs, 13, 14

Springs Hotel Resort, *12*, 13-27, *14*, *15*, *17*, *20*
Squirrel and Dumplings, 25
Squirrel Stew, 24
St. Louis, 2
St. Ores, Viola Musgrove, 65
Stansbury, John, xvi
Stark family, 124
Steph, xv
Stew, 68
Sutton, Ruby, xvi
Sweet Potato Casserole, 7
Sweet Potato Pie Deluxe, 169

T
Texas and New Orleans Railroad, 2, 109
Thanksgiving, 160
Thomas, Otis, 46, 48, 49, 50, *51*, 52
Thompson, Houston, 30
Thornton, Inez, xv
Timber Charlie, xi
Tomato-Cheese Salad, 53
Top Half Cafe, xii, xiv
Topeka, Kansas, 50
Trinity, xvi, 73-78
Tyler County, xviii, 109

U
Udall, Stewart, 146
Uncle Yank, xiii-xiv

V
Vanilla Custard Ice Cream 69
Vegetables:
  Baked Deviled Eggplant Casserole, 166

Baked Sweet Potatoes, 136
Country-Style Hominy, 116
Creamed Stewed Onions, 135
French-Fried Onions, 45
Fresh Shelled Peas, 69
Fried Hominy, 116
Mashed Potatoes, 58
Okra and Tomatoes, 81
Sauerkraut, 117
Sweet Potato Casserole, 7
Venison Chili, 23
Venison Roast, 23
Vickers, Anna, 3
Vickers, Bertha, 3
Vickers, Kate, 3
Village Creek, xii, 139, 165
Vinegar Pie, 83
Vines Hotel, *138*, 139-155, *140*

W
Waco, Beaumont, Trinity and
    Sabine Railroad, 109
West, Minnie, 124
White Sauce, 55
Williford family, 5
Willis, Mrs. P. J., 17
Winnfield, Louisiana, 36
Woodell family, 110
Woodell, Mrs. Evander, 110
Woodville, 2, 109, 111-112, 176
Wright, Lon, 47

Y
Yankie, Ella, 3
Yarborough, Ralph, 146
Yeast Rolls, 44
Yellow Pine Mill, 109

Z
Zesty Appetizer, 53